LinkedIn Sales Mastery: Unlocking Profitable Leads and Dominating the Global Market

By

Prasenjit Sarkar

Introduction

In today's fast-paced and interconnected business landscape, harnessing the power of social media platforms is paramount to success. Among these platforms, LinkedIn stands tall as the ultimate hub for professionals seeking to expand their networks, build lucrative connections, and drive substantial business growth.

In his groundbreaking book, **"LinkedIn Sales Mastery: Unlocking Profitable Leads and Dominating the Global Market,"** author and sales expert, Mr. Prasenjit Sarkar, unveils a comprehensive guide to maximising the potential of LinkedIn as a game-changing sales tool. Drawing on his years of experience and expertise, Sarkar provides invaluable insights, strategies, and techniques that will empower both seasoned professionals and aspiring entrepreneurs to navigate the complex world of LinkedIn with finesse.

Through this captivating journey, you will discover the secrets to unlocking profitable leads and establishing an unparalleled presence in the global market. From leveraging LinkedIn's powerful features and tools to creating compelling content that resonates with your target audience, this book equips you with the knowledge and skills needed to revolutionize your sales approach and achieve remarkable results.

Whether you are a sales executive, business owner, or aspiring professional, "LinkedIn Sales Mastery" serves as your compass, guiding you towards unrivalled success in the digital realm. With Sarkar's practical advice, proven strategies, and real-world examples, you will gain a competitive edge, amplify your reach, and dominate the global market like never before. Prepare to embark on a transformational journey, as Mr. Prasenjit Sarkar invites you to unlock the full potential of LinkedIn, harness profitable leads, and claim your rightful position at the forefront of the ever-evolving business landscape. Get ready to write your success story, one connection at a time.

Table of Contents

Chapter 1: The Art of Prospecting on LinkedIn

Chapter 2: Building an Irresistible Personal Brand

Chapter 3: Nurturing Relationships for Long-Term Success

Chapter 4: Leveraging LinkedIn Groups for Targeted Engagement

Chapter 5: Mastering LinkedIn Sales Navigator

Chapter 6: Creating Compelling Content for LinkedIn

Chapter 7: Maximizing LinkedIn Advertising Opportunities

Chapter 8: Harnessing LinkedIn Analytics for Data-Driven Success

Chapter 9: Expanding Your Reach with LinkedIn Influencers

Chapter 10: Strategies for Global Expansion on LinkedIn

Chapter 11: Advanced Networking Techniques for LinkedIn Success

Chapter 12: LinkedIn as a Sales Funnel: From Lead to Conversion

Chapter 1: The Art of Prospecting on LinkedIn

In this chapter, we dive deep into the art of prospecting on LinkedIn, uncovering proven strategies that will enable you to identify and connect with high-quality leads. Prospecting is the foundation of successful sales on LinkedIn, and mastering this art is essential for unlocking profitable leads and dominating the global market.

The Power of Targeted Prospecting

Effective prospecting begins with a clear understanding of your target audience. By identifying your ideal customers, you can narrow down your search and focus your efforts on connecting with those who are most likely to be interested in your

products or services. LinkedIn offers powerful search features that allow you to filter results based on industry, job title, location, and more, giving you the ability to reach the right people at the right time.

Strategies for Advanced Search

To maximize your prospecting efforts, leverage LinkedIn's advanced search capabilities. Use Boolean operators, such as AND, OR, and NOT, to refine your search queries and find specific combinations of criteria. Combine different filters to create highly targeted searches that yield relevant results. Additionally, save your search criteria to receive regular updates on new prospects who meet your specified criteria, ensuring you stay ahead of the game.

In the realm of prospecting on LinkedIn, mastering the art of advanced search is a game-changer. With LinkedIn's robust search capabilities, you can uncover hidden gems and find highly targeted prospects to fuel your sales efforts. In this section, we will explore proven strategies for leveraging advanced search on LinkedIn to enhance your prospecting game.

1. Utilise Keywords and Boolean Operators

To conduct precise searches, it's important to use relevant keywords and Boolean operators effectively. Start by brainstorming a list of keywords that align with your target audience and industry. Then, combine these keywords using operators such as **"AND," "OR,"** and **"NOT"** to refine your search results. For example, searching for "sales manager AND technology" will narrow down your results to profiles that include both terms.

2. Leverage Filters and Segments

LinkedIn offers various filters and segments to narrow down your search results further. These filters allow you to focus on specific criteria such as location, industry, job title, company size, and more. Utilise these filters to tailor your search to your ideal prospects. Refining your search based on specific criteria will help you uncover highly relevant leads and save time in the prospecting process.

3. Save and Track Search Results

Once you've crafted a targeted search, don't forget to save it for future reference. LinkedIn allows you to save your search criteria, and it will automatically update you with new results that match your search parameters. This feature is particularly useful for ongoing prospecting efforts and staying up-to-date with potential leads.

4. Engage with Insights from Search Results

When you conduct a search on LinkedIn, pay attention to the insights and information provided in the search results. Take note of mutual connections, shared interests, or common groups you have with potential prospects. These insights can be valuable conversation starters and provide a way to establish a meaningful connection right from the start.

5. Follow and Monitor Targeted Prospects

If you come across promising prospects during your search, consider following their profiles to stay updated on their activities. This allows you to monitor their posts, engagements, and content, providing you with valuable insights into their interests and pain points. Engaging with their content strategically can help you build familiarity and nurture the relationship over time.

6. Leverage Saved Searches for Lead Nurturing

Saved searches not only help you find potential prospects but also serve as a powerful tool for lead nurturing. Regularly review your saved searches to identify new leads or changes in your target audience. Reach out to these leads with personalised messages and tailored content, showcasing your understanding of their specific needs. This proactive approach can help you establish yourself as a trusted advisor and accelerate the sales process.

7. Stay Updated with LinkedIn Alerts

LinkedIn alerts are notifications that keep you informed about updates and activities related to your connections and saved searches. Set up relevant alerts to stay on top of industry news, job changes, or company updates. Being aware of these changes allows you to reach out to prospects at opportune moments, positioning yourself as a valuable resource.

Crafting Personalized Messages

Once you have identified potential leads, the next step is to engage them through personalized messages. Avoid generic templates and instead take the time to research and understand each prospect's background, interests, and pain points. Tailor your messages to address their specific needs and demonstrate how your product or service can provide a solution. Personalization is key to capturing the attention of your prospects and fostering meaningful connections.

The Art of Effective Messaging

When crafting your messages, it's crucial to strike a balance between professionalism and personalization. Start with a strong, attention-grabbing subject line that piques the recipient's interest. Introduce yourself and establish credibility by highlighting relevant experiences or mutual connections. Clearly articulate the value proposition of your offering and explain how it aligns with the prospect's goals or challenges. End your message with a compelling call-to-action that encourages further engagement.

Leveraging Warm Introductions and Referrals

One of the most powerful ways to build trust and credibility on LinkedIn is through warm introductions and referrals. Utilize your existing network to identify common connections with your target prospects. Request introductions from mutual connections who can vouch for your expertise and recommend your services. Warm introductions significantly increase the likelihood of successful engagement and conversions.

Cultivating Relationships with Influencers

LinkedIn influencers can play a significant role in your prospecting efforts. Identify influential individuals in your industry who have a large following and engage with their content. Comment thoughtfully on their posts, share valuable insights, and build rapport. Establishing relationships with influencers can help expand your network and position you as a trusted authority, thereby attracting more leads and opportunities.

Engaging with LinkedIn Groups

LinkedIn Groups provide a valuable platform for targeted engagement and lead generation. Join relevant groups in your industry or niche and actively participate in discussions. Share valuable content, offer insights, and contribute to meaningful conversations. By establishing yourself as a knowledgeable and helpful member, you can attract the attention of potential leads and position yourself as an industry expert.

Strategies for Group Engagement

To maximize your impact within LinkedIn Groups, focus on quality over quantity. Select a few groups that align closely with your target audience and actively engage with them. Be consistent in your participation and provide value through insightful comments, sharing valuable resources, and offering assistance to group members. By building relationships and establishing yourself as a trusted resource, you can generate leads and expand your network.

Strategies for Group Engagement

Engaging with LinkedIn groups is a powerful prospecting technique that can significantly expand your reach and establish your expertise in your industry. In this subtopic, we will explore proven strategies for effectively engaging with LinkedIn groups to enhance your prospecting efforts.

Understanding the Dynamics of LinkedIn Groups

Before diving into strategies, it's important to understand the dynamics of

LinkedIn groups. LinkedIn groups bring together professionals with similar interests, industries, or goals. They provide a platform for discussions, knowledge-sharing, and networking. By joining relevant groups, you gain access to a community of like-minded individuals and potential prospects.

1. Identify and Join Relevant Groups

The first step is to identify and join LinkedIn groups that align with your target audience and industry. Look for groups with active discussions and a substantial number of members. Consider the following criteria when selecting groups:

- **Relevance:** Ensure the group's topic is directly related to your industry or target audience.

- **Activity:** Look for groups with regular discussions, engagement, and recent activity.
- **Size:** While group size isn't the sole indicator of quality, larger groups usually offer more networking opportunities.

2. Observe and Understand Group Dynamics

Once you join a group, take the time to observe and understand the group dynamics. Pay attention to the following:

- **Topics and Discussions:** Take note of the common topics and discussions within the group. Identify the pain points, challenges, and trends being discussed.
- **Influencers and Active Members:** Identify the influential members and active participants in the group.

Observe their contributions and engagement patterns.
- **Group Rules and Guidelines:** Familiarize yourself with the group's rules and guidelines to ensure your engagement aligns with the group's expectations.

3. Provide Value through Knowledge Sharing

Engaging with LinkedIn groups is not just about promoting your products or services. It's about building relationships and establishing yourself as a valuable resource. Here are strategies to provide value through knowledge sharing:

- **Share Insights and Expertise:** Contribute to group discussions by sharing valuable insights, industry trends, and expert advice. Be generous with your knowledge and aim to genuinely help others.

- **Answer Questions:** Monitor group discussions for questions related to your expertise. Offer helpful and informative responses, demonstrating your expertise and building credibility.
- **Share Relevant Content:** Share relevant articles, blog posts, or resources that provide value to group members. Ensure the content is informative, well-written, and aligns with the group's interests.

4. Engage Actively and Consistently

Active and consistent engagement is key to building relationships and expanding your network within LinkedIn groups. Consider the following strategies:

- **Initiate Discussions:** Start meaningful discussions by posing thought-provoking questions or sharing interesting industry news. Encourage group members to participate and share their perspectives.
- **Comment and Contribute:** Engage with existing discussions by commenting on posts, asking follow-up questions, and providing additional insights. Add value to the conversation and show genuine interest in others' opinions.
- **Network and Connect:** Actively network with other group members who align with your target audience or have complementary expertise. Send connection requests with personalized messages to initiate further conversations.

5. Respect Group Etiquette and Build Relationships

To effectively engage with LinkedIn groups, it's important to respect group etiquette and focus on relationship-building:

- **Be Respectful:** Treat all group members with respect, even if you disagree with their opinions. Maintain a professional and courteous tone in your interactions.
- **Avoid Self-Promotion:** While it's acceptable to share your expertise, avoid excessive self-promotion or direct sales pitches. Focus on building relationships and establishing yourself as a valuable resource.
- **Connect Personally:** When you find individuals who align with your target audience or have potential business

opportunities, reach out personally to connect. Send personalized messages explaining your interest in connecting and how you can mutually benefit from the relationship.

By implementing these strategies, you can effectively engage with LinkedIn groups and leverage them as a powerful prospecting tool. Remember, successful group engagement is about providing value, building relationships, and establishing yourself as a trusted industry expert.

Summary

This Chapter of "LinkedIn Sales Mastery: Unlocking Profitable Leads and Dominating the Global Market" explores the art of prospecting on LinkedIn. By implementing the proven strategies outlined in this chapter, you can effectively identify and connect with high-quality leads. From utilizing advanced search features to crafting personalized messages, leveraging warm introductions, engaging with influencers, and participating in LinkedIn Groups, these strategies will set you on the path to prospecting success. With a focused and targeted approach, you can unlock profitable leads and dominate the global market on LinkedIn.

Chapter 2: Building an Irresistible Personal Brand

In this chapter, we delve into the importance of building an irresistible personal brand on LinkedIn and provide you with proven strategies to establish yourself as a trusted authority in your industry. Your personal brand is your unique identity on the platform, and it plays a crucial role in attracting profitable leads and dominating the global market.

The Power of Personal Branding on LinkedIn

Personal branding is about showcasing your expertise, establishing credibility, and differentiating yourself from the competition. On LinkedIn, your profile serves as the foundation of your personal brand. It is essential to optimize your profile to make a strong and lasting impression on visitors and potential leads.

Defining Your Personal Brand

To harness the power of personal branding on LinkedIn, you must first define and articulate your personal brand. Here are some essential steps to get started:

1. Identify Your Unique Value Proposition

Determine what makes you stand out from the crowd. Reflect on your expertise, experiences, and strengths. Identify the specific skills and knowledge that set you apart and align with your target audience's needs. For example, if you're a marketing professional, you might have a deep understanding of content marketing strategies or a knack for creating viral campaigns.

2. Craft a Compelling Personal Brand Statement

Create a concise and compelling personal brand statement that communicates who you are, what you do, and the value you bring. This statement should resonate with your target audience and capture their attention. For instance, a personal brand statement for a social media consultant might be: **"Helping businesses amplify their online presence and drive meaningful engagement through strategic social media marketing."**

3. Define Your Brand Voice and Visual Identity

Develop a consistent brand voice and visual identity that aligns with your personal brand. Your brand voice should reflect your personality and values, and your visual identity should be visually appealing and professional. For example, if you want to position yourself as an authoritative industry expert, your brand voice might be informative and confident, and your visual identity might incorporate professional headshots and a clean, modern design aesthetic.

Building Your Personal Brand on LinkedIn

Now that you have defined your personal brand, it's time to build and cultivate it on LinkedIn. Here are some proven strategies to help you establish a compelling personal brand presence on the platform:

1. Optimise Your LinkedIn Profile

Your LinkedIn profile is your personal brand's digital representation, so it's crucial to optimise it for maximum impact. Use your personal brand statement as your headline and craft a compelling summary that showcases your expertise, achievements, and value proposition. Highlight relevant skills, experiences, and certifications. Include multimedia elements such as videos, presentations, or projects to provide evidence of your expertise.

2. Share Thoughtful and Relevant Content

Consistently share valuable and insightful content that aligns with your personal brand and resonates with your target audience. Write articles, create informative videos, or curate relevant industry news and insights. Be authentic and provide unique perspectives or actionable tips that showcase your expertise. Engage with your audience by asking thought-provoking questions and responding to comments promptly.

3. Engage in Meaningful Conversations

Actively participate in relevant LinkedIn groups, industry communities, and professional conversations. Contribute to discussions, offer valuable insights, and connect with like-minded professionals. Engaging in meaningful conversations demonstrates your expertise and builds your network. For instance, if you're a cybersecurity professional, you can join cybersecurity-related groups and share your knowledge on best practices and emerging threats.

Examples of Personal Branding Success on LinkedIn

To illustrate the power of personal branding on LinkedIn, let's explore a couple of examples:

1. Sarah Thompson - The Sustainable Fashion Advocate

Sarah Thompson, a fashion entrepreneur and sustainability

advocate, has built a powerful personal brand on LinkedIn. Through her thoughtfully crafted articles and engaging videos, she educates her audience about the importance of sustainable fashion and its positive impact on the environment. Sarah's personal brand statement highlights her expertise in sustainable fashion and her mission to transform the industry. Her authentic and passionate approach has attracted a dedicated following and led to speaking opportunities at industry conferences.

2. James Anderson - The Financial Wellness Expert

James Anderson, a financial planner and wellness advocate, has established himself as a trusted authority on LinkedIn. He consistently shares practical tips and advice on achieving financial wellness, addressing topics such as budgeting, investments, and retirement planning. James actively engages with his audience by hosting live Q&A sessions and responding to comments with personalized recommendations. His personal brand exudes reliability and empathy, positioning him as a go-to resource for financial guidance.

Crafting an Engaging Headline and Summary

Your headline and summary are the first elements that visitors see when they land on your profile. Craft a compelling headline that clearly communicates your value proposition and captures attention. Use keywords relevant to your industry to increase your visibility in search results. In the summary section, tell a captivating brand story that highlights your experience, skills, and unique selling points. Clearly articulate how you can provide value to your target audience.

Why Your Headline and Summary Matter

Your headline and summary are often the first things people see when they come across your profile. They play a crucial role in capturing attention, generating interest, and enticing individuals to learn more about you. A well-crafted headline and summary can differentiate you from the competition and pique curiosity, leading to more profile views, connection requests, and potential career opportunities.

Crafting an Engaging Headline

Your headline should succinctly convey who you are, what you do, and the unique value you bring. It should be compelling, keyword-rich, and tailored to your target audience. Consider incorporating relevant industry buzzwords, accomplishments, or a unique selling point that sets you apart. For example:

- Dynamic Marketing Strategist | Helping Businesses Drive Growth through Innovative Digital Campaigns
- Experienced Sales Professional | Delivering Revenue-Boosting Solutions for B2B Enterprises

- Passionate Environmental Advocate | Working Towards a Sustainable Future

By customising your headline to align with your expertise and the needs of your target audience, you can capture their attention and make a strong first impression.

Crafting an Informative Summary

Your summary provides an opportunity to elaborate on your professional background, highlight key achievements, and showcase your unique skills and qualifications. It should be concise, engaging, and easy to read. Here are some strategies to consider when crafting your summary:

1. **Tell Your Story:** Use storytelling techniques to engage readers and create an emotional connection.

Share experiences, challenges, and how they shaped your professional journey. For example:

As a child, I was captivated by the power of technology. This passion led me to pursue a career in software engineering, where I have spent the past decade developing innovative solutions that streamline business operations and drive efficiency.

2. **Highlight Achievements:** Showcase your notable accomplishments and quantify them whenever possible. This helps establish credibility and demonstrates your expertise. For instance:

Throughout my career, I have successfully led cross-functional teams, resulting in a 20% increase

in project efficiency and a 15% reduction in costs.

3. **Focus on Value:** Clearly articulate the value you bring to potential employers or clients. Identify their pain points and explain how you can provide solutions. Use language that resonates with your target audience. For **example:**

   I am dedicated to helping businesses enhance their online presence and reach their target audience effectively. **By leveraging my expertise in digital marketing and data analytics, I have helped numerous clients achieve a 30% increase in website traffic and a 25% boost in conversion rates.**

4. **Include Relevant Keywords:** Incorporate industry-specific keywords throughout your summary

to optimise your profile for search. This increases the chances of being discovered by recruiters or clients looking for specific skills or expertise. Remember, your headline and summary should be authentic reflections of your professional identity. They should not only highlight your skills and achievements but also convey your unique personality and passion for what you do.

Examples of Compelling Headlines and Summaries

To illustrate the power of well-crafted headlines and summaries, let's explore a few examples:

Example 1:

Headline: *Results-Driven Project Manager | Delivering Seamless*

Operations and Exceeding Client Expectations

Summary: *With a proven track record of successfully managing complex projects across diverse industries, I excel in driving operational excellence and exceeding client expectations. From project initiation to successful delivery, I am committed to ensuring seamless operations, fostering cross-functional collaboration, and delivering results that propel business growth. Let's connect and explore how I can contribute to your organisation's success.*

Example 2:

Headline: *Creative Graphic Designer | Transforming Ideas into Visually Stunning Designs*

Summary: *As a passionate and innovative graphic designer, I have a* knack for transforming ideas into visually stunning designs that captivate audiences. With expertise in Adobe Creative Suite and an eye for detail, I bring concepts to life through compelling visuals that leave a lasting impact. Let's collaborate on your next design project and create something extraordinary.

Example 3:

Headline: *Experienced Financial Analyst | Driving Data-Driven Decision Making and Maximising ROI*

Summary: *With a strong background in financial analysis and a deep understanding of market trends, I empower businesses to make informed, data-driven decisions that maximise return on investment. Through meticulous financial modelling, risk assessment, and performance* *evaluation, I provide strategic insights that drive profitability and sustainable growth. Let's discuss how I can contribute to your financial success.*

By studying these examples, you can see how each headline succinctly communicates the professional identity and value proposition, while the summaries expand on the skills, achievements, and value that the individual brings to the table.

Craft your headline and summary with care, ensuring they accurately represent your unique professional brand and resonate with your target audience. Remember, these elements will play a pivotal role in attracting the right connections and opportunities on LinkedIn.

Showcasing Your Expertise

To build an irresistible personal brand, you must demonstrate your expertise and establish yourself as a thought leader in your industry. LinkedIn offers several features and strategies to showcase your knowledge and skills effectively. This section will explore proven strategies for effectively demonstrating your knowledge, skills, and experience to enhance your personal brand on LinkedIn.

1. Publish High-Quality Content

One of the most powerful ways to showcase your expertise is by consistently publishing high-quality content on LinkedIn. This can include articles, blog posts, or even short-form posts. Share valuable insights, industry trends, and practical tips that resonate with your target audience. Make sure your content is well-researched, informative, and provides unique perspectives to set yourself apart from others in your field.

Example: If you're a marketing professional, you could write an article on the latest digital marketing strategies and how they can drive business growth. Share real-life case studies and actionable advice to demonstrate your expertise and provide value to your audience.

2. Engage in Thoughtful Discussions

Engaging in thoughtful discussions on LinkedIn is an excellent way to showcase your expertise and build credibility. Join relevant industry groups and actively participate in conversations. Offer valuable insights, answer questions, and provide solutions to challenges raised by other professionals. By demonstrating your knowledge and willingness to contribute, you position yourself as a trusted authority in your field.

Example: Suppose you're a cybersecurity expert. Engage in discussions on topics such as data privacy, cyber threats, or best practices for securing networks. Share your expertise, share relevant resources, and engage in meaningful conversations with other professionals in the cybersecurity community.

3. Obtain Recommendations and Endorsements

Recommendations and endorsements from colleagues, clients, or industry leaders can significantly boost your credibility on LinkedIn. Request recommendations from people you've worked with closely and who can vouch for your expertise and the value you bring. Endorsements for specific skills further validate your capabilities and expertise in those areas. These testimonials provide social proof of your abilities and enhance your personal brand.

Example: Let's say you're a project manager. Request recommendations from clients or team members who have witnessed your exceptional project management skills in action. Their testimonials can highlight your ability to deliver projects on time, manage resources effectively, and communicate clearly, reinforcing your expertise in project management.

4. Participate in Webinars and Industry Events

Participating in webinars and industry events is an effective way to showcase your expertise to a broader audience. Look for speaking opportunities or panel discussions where you can share your insights and knowledge. Engage with the audience, answer questions, and provide valuable takeaways. The exposure gained from such events can elevate your personal brand and attract new connections and opportunities.

Example: Suppose you're an **HR professional** specializing in employee engagement. Offer to speak at a virtual HR conference on the topic of fostering employee well-being and motivation in the remote work era. Share practical strategies, real-life examples, and engage with the audience to position yourself as an expert in the field of employee engagement.

5. Curate and Share Industry News

Demonstrate your expertise by staying updated with the latest industry news and trends. Curate relevant articles, reports, and studies and share them with your network. Add your insights and commentary to showcase your understanding of industry developments. By consistently sharing valuable and insightful content, you establish yourself as a knowledgeable professional with a finger on the pulse of your industry.

Example: If you're a **finance professional**, share news articles about the impact of regulatory changes on the financial industry or provide an analysis of market trends. Offer your unique perspective and explain how these developments may affect businesses or individuals, demonstrating your expertise in finance.

Remember, showcasing your expertise on LinkedIn is an ongoing process. Consistently share valuable content, engage in meaningful discussions, seek recommendations, participate in events, and stay updated with industry news. By actively demonstrating your knowledge and skills, you'll establish yourself as a trusted authority in your field and build an irresistible personal brand on LinkedIn.

Publishing Thought-Provoking Content

Thought-provoking content not only captures the attention of your audience but also establishes you as a knowledgeable and influential professional in your industry. By sharing valuable insights, engaging stories, and actionable advice, you can position yourself as a thought leader and attract a loyal following. Let's delve into the strategies and examples that will help you publish thought-provoking content and elevate your personal brand on LinkedIn.

The Power of Thought-Provoking Content

Thought-provoking content is the backbone of establishing your personal brand on LinkedIn. It is content that challenges conventional wisdom, sparks conversations, and provides fresh perspectives. Here's why it's essential:

1. **Capturing Attention:** In the vast sea of content on LinkedIn, thought-provoking content stands out. It captures attention and piques the curiosity of your audience, enticing them to read, engage, and share your posts.

2. **Establishing Authority:** Publishing thought-provoking content demonstrates your expertise and authority in your field. It positions you as a knowledgeable professional who is at the forefront of industry trends and innovations.

3. **Driving Engagement:** Thought-provoking content encourages meaningful discussions and engagement. When you share

ideas that resonate with your audience, they are more likely to comment, share their opinions, and participate in conversations, thereby increasing your visibility and reach.

Strategies for Publishing Thought-Provoking Content

To create and share thought-provoking content that resonates with your audience, consider the following strategies:

1. Identify Relevant Topics

Stay up-to-date with industry news, trends, and challenges. Identify topics that are relevant to your target audience and align with your expertise. Look for gaps in existing conversations and seek opportunities to offer unique insights.

2. Provide Valuable Insights

When crafting your content, aim to provide valuable insights and actionable advice. Share your knowledge, experiences, and lessons learned. Offer practical tips, best practices, and strategies that your audience can implement in their own work or lives.

3. Tell Compelling Stories

Stories have the power to captivate and inspire. Incorporate storytelling techniques into your content to make it relatable and engaging. Share personal anecdotes, case studies, or client success stories that demonstrate the impact of your expertise.

4. Encourage Discussion and Debate

Invite your audience to engage in meaningful conversations by posing thought-provoking questions or asking for their opinions on controversial topics. Create a safe and respectful space for different viewpoints, and actively participate in the discussions to foster engagement.

5. Use Visuals and Multimedia

Enhance the impact of your content by incorporating visuals such as infographics, charts, or images. Consider using multimedia formats like videos or podcasts to provide a diverse and engaging experience for your audience.

Examples of Thought-Provoking Content

Let's explore some examples of thought-provoking content that can inspire your own creations:

1. **"The Future of Artificial Intelligence in Marketing"**: In this post, you can share your insights on how AI is transforming the marketing landscape and discuss its potential implications for businesses. Encourage your audience to consider the ethical aspects and share their opinions on AI's role in marketing strategy.
2. **"Why Failure is the Path to Success"**: Share your personal experiences and lessons learned from failures. Discuss how embracing failure can lead to personal growth and innovation. Encourage your audience to share their own stories of overcoming failure and the lessons they gained from them.

3. **"Unconventional Strategies for Boosting Employee Productivity"**: Challenge traditional productivity norms by sharing unconventional strategies that have worked for you or your clients. Encourage your audience to question established practices and explore new approaches to enhance productivity.

Remember, thought-provoking content should aim to spark meaningful conversations and provide value to your audience. Use these examples as inspiration, but ensure that your content reflects your unique perspective and expertise.

Sharing Engaging Updates

In addition to publishing articles, sharing regular updates on LinkedIn is a powerful way to maintain visibility and demonstrate your expertise. Share industry news, trends, and relevant insights. Add your unique perspective and spark discussions in the comments section. Engage with your network by providing value through your updates, fostering meaningful conversations, and attracting the attention of potential leads. This section will explore proven strategies for sharing updates that spark conversations, drive engagement, and elevate your personal brand on LinkedIn.

Why Sharing Engaging Updates Matters

Sharing engaging updates is a powerful way to showcase your expertise, establish credibility, and attract the attention of your LinkedIn network.

When you consistently provide valuable and relevant content, you position yourself as a go-to resource in your field. This helps to build trust with your connections, attract new followers, and ultimately expand your professional network.

Tips for Creating Engaging Updates

1. Focus on Quality and Relevance: Share updates that are informative, insightful, and relevant to your industry or area of expertise. Aim to provide value to your audience by sharing industry news, expert opinions, tips and tricks, or thought-provoking questions.
Example: If you are a **digital marketing expert,** you could share an update about the latest trends in social media advertising or provide

tips on creating effective email marketing campaigns.
2. **Use Visuals to Enhance Impact:** Incorporate eye-catching visuals such as images, infographics, or videos in your updates. Visual content tends to attract more attention and engagement compared to text-only posts.
Example: If you are sharing a statistic or a data-driven insight, create an infographic to present the information in a visually appealing and easy-to-understand format.
3. **Craft Compelling Headlines:** Pay attention to your updated headlines as they serve as the first impression to capture your audience's attention. Craft clear, concise, and compelling headlines that entice users to click and read more.

Example: Instead of a generic headline like **"New Marketing Strategy,"** opt for something more intriguing and specific like **"Unleashing the Power of User-Generated Content: A Revolutionary Marketing Strategy."**

4. **Encourage Engagement and Conversation:** End your updates with a clear **call-to-action** that encourages your audience to engage and share their thoughts. Ask questions, seek opinions, or invite users to share their own experiences related to the topic.

Example: After sharing a post about the importance of work-life balance, you could end with a question like, **"What are your favourite strategies for maintaining a healthy work-life**

balance? Share your tips in the comments below!"

5. **Timing and Consistency:** Consider the timing of your updates to maximise visibility and engagement. Research your target audience's online behaviour and identify the times when they are most active on LinkedIn. Additionally, be consistent in your posting frequency to stay on top of your audience's minds.

Example: If you find that your target audience is most active on LinkedIn during weekday evenings, schedule your updates to go live during those times to reach a larger audience.

Real-Life Examples

To illustrate the impact of sharing engaging updates, let's look at a few real-life examples of professionals who have effectively built their personal brands on LinkedIn:

1. John Mitchell, **a leadership coach**, regularly shares insightful updates on topics such as effective communication, team building, and personal growth. His updates often include practical tips and actionable advice that resonate with his audience. By consistently providing valuable content, John has attracted a large following and established himself as a trusted authority in his field.

2. Sarah Patel, **a graphic designer,** uses visual content to showcase her creativity and expertise. She shares before-and-after design examples, tips for creating visually appealing graphics, and industry trends.

Sarah's visually engaging updates have helped her gain visibility within the design community and attract clients who appreciate her unique style.

3. Mark Thompson, **a technology consultant**, focuses on sharing updates about emerging technologies, industry insights, and best practices. His updates often spark discussions and debates among his connections, positioning him as a thought leader and a go-to resource for technology-related topics. Mark's engaging updates have opened doors to speaking opportunities and collaboration with other industry experts.

These examples highlight the power of sharing engaging updates in building a strong personal brand on LinkedIn. By following the strategies mentioned above and leveraging your expertise, you can create a compelling online presence that sets you apart from the competition.

Cultivating a Strong Online Presence

A strong online presence goes beyond your LinkedIn profile. It encompasses your activity and engagement on the platform, as well as your presence on other digital channels.

Building Relationships through Engagement

Engagement is key to building a strong online presence on LinkedIn. Actively participate in conversations, comment on others' posts, and share valuable insights. Be authentic and genuine in your interactions. Respond promptly to comments on your own posts, fostering meaningful discussions and creating a sense of community. By consistently engaging with your network, you build relationships, increase your visibility, and attract potential leads.

Establishing a Cross-Channel Presence

LinkedIn is not the only platform where you can showcase your personal brand. Consider extending your presence to other relevant digital channels such as your website, blog, or other social media platforms. Create a cohesive brand experience across these channels by maintaining consistent messaging, visual elements, and brand voice. Link back to your LinkedIn profile to drive traffic and expand your network. In this section, we will explore the importance of establishing a cross-channel presence and provide practical strategies to help you achieve it.

Why Establish a Cross-Channel Presence?

Building a personal brand across multiple channels offers several benefits. Firstly, it allows you to expand your reach and connect with a broader audience. Different people prefer different platforms, so by being present on various channels, you increase the chances of reaching and engaging with potential followers and customers. Secondly, a cross-channel presence provides versatility in terms of content formats. Each platform has its own strengths and limitations, allowing you to showcase different aspects of your expertise. For example, LinkedIn may be ideal for sharing professional insights and networking, while Instagram allows for more visual storytelling. By utilising multiple channels, you can leverage these unique features to present a well-rounded personal brand.

Lastly, a cross-channel presence builds credibility and reinforces your personal brand's consistency. When your audience sees you active and engaged on various platforms, it creates a perception of expertise and reliability. It demonstrates that you are committed to providing value across different channels, further strengthening your brand reputation.

Strategies for Establishing a Cross-Channel Presence

To establish a successful cross-channel presence, consider the following strategies:

1. Identify Suitable Platforms: Begin by identifying the platforms that align with your personal brand and target audience. Research where your ideal audience spends their time and which platforms best showcase your expertise. This could include LinkedIn, Twitter, Instagram, YouTube, or even industry-specific forums or communities.

2. Adapt Content for Each Platform: Each platform has its own unique characteristics, user demographics, and content formats. Tailor your content to suit the platform while maintaining consistency in your brand voice and messaging. For example, on LinkedIn, you might focus on sharing professional articles and engaging in industry discussions, while on Instagram, you can highlight your visual portfolio or behind-the-scenes moments.

3. Cross-Promote and Repurpose Content: Maximise your efforts by cross-promoting your content across platforms. For instance, share a snippet of a YouTube video on LinkedIn with a link to the full video. Similarly, repurpose your blog posts into short, engaging threads on Twitter or create visually appealing infographics for Instagram.

4. Engage with Your Audience: Building a cross-channel presence requires active engagement with your audience. Respond to comments, participate in discussions, and initiate conversations. Show genuine interest and provide value to your followers, regardless of the platform. By fostering meaningful connections, you establish yourself as a trusted authority in your field.

5. Track Analytics and Iterate:
Regularly monitor analytics and insights provided by each platform. Pay attention to engagement metrics, reach, and audience demographics. Use this data to identify which channels are most effective in reaching your target audience and adjust your strategy accordingly. Experiment with different types of content and measure their impact to continually improve your cross-channel presence.

Example: Establishing a Cross-Channel Presence

Let's consider the example of Sarah, a marketing consultant aiming to build her personal brand. Sarah identifies LinkedIn, Twitter, and her own blog as suitable platforms to establish her cross-channel presence.

On LinkedIn, Sarah regularly shares industry insights, contributes to relevant discussions, and engages with professionals in her field. She showcases her expertise through thought-provoking articles and by providing valuable comments on other people's posts. Sarah also utilises LinkedIn Live to host webinars and engage with her audience in real-time.

On Twitter, Sarah focuses on sharing bite-sized marketing tips, participating in relevant Twitter chats, and following industry influencers. She actively responds to tweets and initiates conversations by asking thought-provoking questions.

Sarah's blog serves as a central hub for her long-form content, including in-depth articles, case studies, and guides. She repurposes her blog content by creating visually appealing infographics and sharing them on Instagram and Pinterest.

By adopting a cross-channel approach, Sarah maximises her reach, showcases different aspects of her expertise, and establishes herself as a credible marketing consultant across multiple platforms. She consistently engages with her audience and adapts her content to suit each platform's unique characteristics.

Leveraging Recommendations and Endorsements

Recommendations and endorsements on LinkedIn are powerful social proofs that can enhance your personal brand. Request recommendations from clients, colleagues, and mentors who can vouch for your skills and expertise. Display these recommendations prominently on your profile to showcase your credibility. Additionally, seek endorsements for specific skills relevant to your industry. This not only validates your expertise but also increases your visibility in search results. By strategically managing and utilizing these features, you can establish credibility, gain trust, and attract a larger audience. Let's delve into the strategies and examples of leveraging recommendations and endorsements effectively.

The Power of Recommendations

Recommendations are personal testimonials from individuals who have worked with you or experienced your services firsthand. They provide insights into your strengths, work ethic, and professionalism. Here's how you can leverage recommendations to enhance your personal brand:

1. **Request Recommendations:** Reach out to previous clients, colleagues, or business partners who can vouch for your skills and ask them to write a recommendation on your LinkedIn profile. Personalize your request, reminding them of specific projects or achievements you worked on together. Highlight the value their recommendation would bring to your profile.

2. **Give to Receive:** A great way to receive recommendations is by giving them first. Take the initiative to write thoughtful and sincere recommendations for individuals you have worked with. This not only strengthens your professional relationships but also increases the likelihood of receiving recommendations in return.
3. **Highlight Specific Achievements:** When requesting recommendations, guide the person by suggesting specific achievements or areas they could focus on. For example, if you excelled in project management, request a recommendation highlighting your exceptional organizational skills and ability to meet deadlines.

4. **Display Recommendations Strategically:** Showcase your best recommendations prominently on your LinkedIn profile. Arrange them strategically, placing the most impactful and relevant recommendations at the top. This provides visitors with immediate social proof of your capabilities and helps strengthen your personal brand.

The Influence of Endorsements

Endorsements on LinkedIn are a way for your connections to validate your skills and expertise with a simple click. While endorsements may not carry the same weight as recommendations, they still play a crucial role in building your personal brand. Here's how to effectively leverage endorsements:

1. **Curate Your Skills:** Carefully select and curate the skills listed on your LinkedIn profile. Focus on those that align with your personal brand and areas where you want to position yourself as an expert. By prioritizing specific skills, you encourage endorsements in those areas.
2. **Promote Relevant Skills:** Actively promote your skills by engaging with your network and demonstrating your expertise. Share insightful articles, provide valuable comments on industry discussions, and contribute to relevant LinkedIn groups. This positions you as a knowledgeable professional and encourages endorsements from connections who recognize your expertise.
3. **Acknowledge Endorsements:** When you receive an endorsement,

take the time to acknowledge and thank the person who endorsed you. Engage in a conversation, express your appreciation, and consider reciprocating the endorsement if it aligns with your experience of their skills.

4. **Seek Endorsements from Influencers:** Aim to receive endorsements from well-known influencers or industry leaders. Their endorsements carry significant weight and can boost your personal brand's visibility and credibility. Engage with influencers by sharing their content, providing valuable insights, and building meaningful relationships.

Examples of Effective Recommendations and Endorsements Usage

To illustrate the power of recommendations and endorsements, let's consider a few examples:

Example 1: Jane, a Freelance Graphic Designer

Jane, a talented **freelance graphic designer**, leverages recommendations and endorsements effectively to strengthen her personal brand. She actively reaches out to her previous clients and colleagues, requesting recommendations that highlight her creativity, attention to detail, and ability to deliver outstanding design projects. Jane also curates her skills on LinkedIn, focusing on graphic design, branding, and user experience. As a result, she receives endorsements from clients, colleagues, and industry professionals who recognize her expertise. These recommendations and endorsements showcase Jane's skills, build trust, and attract new clients to her freelance business.

Example 2: Mark, a Marketing Consultant

Mark, **a marketing consultant**, strategically manages recommendations and endorsements to establish himself as an authority in his field. He consistently delivers exceptional results for his clients and proactively requests recommendations that emphasize his strategic thinking, data analysis skills, and marketing campaign success. Mark curates his skills to highlight marketing strategy, digital advertising, and market research. He engages with industry influencers by sharing their content, adding valuable insights, and building relationships. This leads to endorsements from influential figures in the marketing industry, strengthening Mark's personal brand and attracting new consulting opportunities.

Summary

Chapter 2 of "LinkedIn Sales Mastery: Unlocking Profitable Leads and Dominating the Global Market" highlights the significance of building an irresistible personal brand on LinkedIn. By implementing the strategies outlined in this chapter, you can establish yourself as a trusted authority, attract profitable leads, and dominate the global market. By optimizing your profile, showcasing your expertise, cultivating a strong online presence, and leveraging social proof, you can create a personal brand that captivates your target audience and sets you apart from the competition.

Chapter 3: Nurturing Relationships for Long-Term Success

In this chapter, we explore the crucial aspect of nurturing relationships on LinkedIn for long-term success. Building strong connections and cultivating meaningful relationships is essential for turning leads into loyal customers and dominating the global market. We provide proven strategies to help you foster long-term relationships and maximize your sales potential on LinkedIn.

The Value of Relationship Building

Relationships are the foundation of successful sales, and LinkedIn offers a unique platform to connect with potential clients, industry peers, and thought leaders. Building genuine relationships enables you to establish trust, understand your customers' needs, and provide tailored solutions. Investing time and effort in nurturing relationships on LinkedIn can lead to long-term partnerships, repeat business, and a strong network of advocates for your brand. we will explore the value of relationship building on LinkedIn and provide strategies to foster genuine connections that can lead to long-term success.

Why Relationship Building Matters on LinkedIn

1. **Trust and Credibility:** Building relationships on LinkedIn helps establish trust and credibility among your connections. When you actively engage with others, share valuable insights, and contribute to meaningful discussions, you position yourself as a knowledgeable and trustworthy professional. This trust and credibility

can open doors to new collaborations, partnerships, and business opportunities.

2. **Networking and Referrals:** LinkedIn is a powerful networking platform, and strong relationships can lead to valuable referrals. When you build strong connections with like-minded professionals and consistently nurture those relationships, they are more likely to refer you to their own network when relevant opportunities arise. These referrals can significantly expand your reach and increase the chances of securing new clients or partnerships.

3. **Industry Influence and Thought Leadership:** By building relationships on LinkedIn, you can establish yourself as an industry

influencer and thought leader. Engaging with others in your field, sharing valuable content, and providing insightful comments can elevate your professional reputation and increase your visibility within your industry. As a result, you become a go-to resource for industry insights, which can attract new connections and opportunities.

4. **Collaboration and Knowledge Sharing:** LinkedIn offers a vast pool of professionals with diverse expertise and backgrounds. By building relationships with individuals who complement your skills and knowledge, you can foster collaboration and tap into collective intelligence. Engaging in discussions, participating in industry groups, and seeking out opportunities for

knowledge sharing can lead to valuable collaborations, joint ventures, and innovative solutions.

Strategies for Effective Relationship Building on LinkedIn

1. **Personalized Connection Requests:** When sending connection requests, take the time to personalize each message. Mention a shared interest, a common connection, or a specific reason for wanting to connect. By demonstrating genuine interest and a thoughtful approach, you increase the likelihood of your request being accepted.
2. **Engagement and Relationship Nurturing:** Actively engage with your connections by liking, commenting, and sharing their posts. Show

appreciation for their contributions and provide meaningful insights. By nurturing these relationships, you build rapport and create a reciprocal environment where others are more likely to engage with your content as well.

3. **Networking Events and Groups:** Participate in LinkedIn networking events and groups relevant to your industry or interests. These platforms offer opportunities to connect with like-minded professionals, exchange ideas, and build relationships with individuals who share common goals. Actively contribute to discussions, share valuable resources, and offer support to foster meaningful connections.

4. **Offering Value:** Always strive to provide value to your connections.

Share informative articles, industry trends, or helpful resources that align with their interests. Offer your expertise and support whenever possible. By consistently providing value, you strengthen your relationships and position yourself as a valuable asset within your network.

5. **Offline Engagement:** While LinkedIn is a digital platform, don't overlook the importance of offline engagement. Connect with your LinkedIn connections through other channels such as email, phone calls, or in-person meetings. These offline interactions can deepen relationships and create opportunities for collaboration beyond the virtual space.

Examples of Effective Relationship Building on LinkedIn

Example 1: John, **a digital marketing professional**, actively engages with his connections by providing valuable insights and commenting on their posts. His expertise and genuine interest in helping others have positioned him as a trusted resource within his industry. As a result, he receives frequent referrals from his network and has secured several high-profile clients.

Example 2: Sarah, **a software developer,** participates in industry-specific LinkedIn groups where she shares her expertise and engages in discussions. Through these interactions, she has connected with professionals from different companies, leading to collaborations on innovative projects. Her relationships built on

LinkedIn have expanded her professional network and opened doors to exciting career opportunities.

Example 3: Mark, **a sales executive,** attends virtual networking events organized by LinkedIn. By actively participating in these events, he has established relationships with key decision-makers in his target industry. These connections have translated into successful partnerships and increased sales for his company.

By applying these strategies and leveraging the power of relationship building on LinkedIn, professionals can create a strong network of trusted connections, unlock new opportunities, and achieve long-term success in their careers or businesses.

Active Listening and Engagement

Active listening is a fundamental skill in relationship building. Pay close attention to your connections' posts, comments, and conversations. Engage genuinely by liking, commenting, and sharing valuable insights. Demonstrate your interest and understanding of their challenges. By actively participating in discussions and providing thoughtful responses, you show your connections that you value their input and are invested in their success. we explore the importance of active listening and engagement on LinkedIn and provide proven strategies to master these skills.

Why Active Listening Matters

Active listening is the art of fully focusing on and comprehending what the other person is saying. It involves giving your undivided attention, being present in the conversation, and demonstrating genuine interest. When it comes to nurturing relationships on LinkedIn, active listening is the key to understanding your connections' pain points, aspirations, and goals. By actively listening, you can gather valuable insights that allow you to tailor your approach and provide relevant solutions.

Strategies for Active Listening and Engagement

1. **Be Present and Responsive:** When engaging with your connections on LinkedIn, give them your undivided attention. Avoid distractions and actively participate in the conversation. Respond promptly to messages, comments, and questions. This shows that you value their input and are committed to

building a meaningful relationship.
Example: If a connection shares an article or a post, take the time to read it thoroughly and provide a thoughtful comment or question that demonstrates your engagement with the content. This not only shows active listening but also sparks further discussion.

2. **Ask Open-Ended Questions:** Engage your connections by asking open-ended questions that encourage them to share more about their experiences, challenges, or goals. Open-ended questions invite detailed responses and provide an opportunity for deeper conversations.
Example: Instead of asking a simple "yes" or "no" question, ask something like, **"What strategies have you found effective in overcoming the**

challenges you mentioned in your recent post?" This allows your connection to share insights and experiences, fostering more meaningful dialogue.

3. **Reflect and Empathize:** Demonstrate empathy by reflecting on what your connections have shared. Repeat key points they've made, summarise their thoughts, and acknowledge their feelings or concerns. This shows that you understand and value their perspective.

   Example: If a connection expresses frustration about a particular industry challenge, respond with empathy and understanding. Acknowledge their concerns and share your own experiences or insights that demonstrate you've truly listened and can relate to their situation.

4. **Provide Value through Knowledge Sharing:** Actively contribute to conversations by sharing your knowledge, expertise, and resources. Be generous with your insights and offer practical solutions or advice. By providing value, you position yourself as a trusted resource and build credibility with your connections.

Example: If a connection asks for recommendations on a certain topic, offer specific suggestions and share relevant articles, podcasts, or tools that can help address their needs. This showcases your expertise and establishes you as a valuable source of information.

5. **Follow up and Follow Through:** Actively nurture relationships by following up on previous conversations and commitments. If you discussed a specific action or promised to share additional information, make sure to follow through. This demonstrates reliability and reinforces the trust you've built with your connections.

Example: If you mentioned during a conversation that you would connect your connection with a relevant contact, make sure to introduce them and follow up to ensure the introduction was valuable. This shows that you are committed to helping them succeed and strengthens the bond between you.

Personalized Outreach and Follow-ups

When nurturing relationships, it's crucial to personalize your outreach and follow-up efforts. Tailor your messages to address specific pain points or interests of your connections. Reference previous conversations or interactions to show that you remember and value the relationship. Follow up regularly to stay top-of-mind and maintain a consistent presence. Personalization and timely follow-ups demonstrate your commitment and build trust over time. Building meaningful connections is key to establishing trust and fostering ongoing engagement with your prospects and clients. By tailoring your outreach messages and following up strategically, you can strengthen relationships, increase response rates, and drive conversions. Let's delve into the strategies and examples that will help you master personalized outreach and follow-ups.

1. Tailoring Your Outreach Messages

When reaching out to prospects or reconnecting with existing connections, generic and impersonal messages are likely to be overlooked or dismissed. Personalized outreach messages demonstrate your genuine interest and understanding of the recipient's needs. Here are some strategies to craft effective personalized messages:

- **Reference Their Profile:** Begin your message by referencing something specific from the recipient's profile that caught your attention. It could be a recent accomplishment, shared interest, or mutual connection. For example:

"Hello [Prospect's Name], I noticed on your LinkedIn profile that you recently launched an innovative product in the healthcare industry. As someone with a passion for healthcare advancements, I would love to learn more about your journey and explore potential collaboration opportunities."

- **Address Pain Points:** Identify the pain points your prospects are facing and address them directly in your message. Offer insights or solutions that demonstrate your expertise and the value you can provide. For example:

"Hi [Prospect's Name], I understand that improving operational efficiency is a top priority for businesses in your industry. With my experience in

streamlining processes and implementing automation solutions, I believe I can help you achieve significant cost savings and enhance productivity."

- **Customize the Call to Action:** Tailor your call to action based on the recipient's current stage in the buyer's journey. Offer a specific next step that aligns with their needs and interests. For example:

"If you're interested, I would be happy to schedule a brief call next week to discuss how our software can streamline your customer service operations. Let me know a convenient time for you, or feel free to book a slot directly on my calendar using the link below."

2. Strategic Follow-ups

Following up with your prospects and clients is crucial for nurturing relationships and staying top-of-mind. However, it's essential to follow up strategically to avoid being perceived as pushy or spammy. Here are some best practices for strategic follow-ups:

- **Timely Response:** Respond promptly to any messages or inquiries you receive. Aim to reply within 24-48 hours to demonstrate your attentiveness and professionalism.
- **Value-Added Follow-ups:** Instead of just checking in or sending generic follow-up messages, provide additional value in each interaction. Share relevant industry insights and useful resources, or invite them to

relevant webinars or events that align with their interests.
- **Reminder of Previous Conversation:** When following up, refer back to any previous conversations or interactions to refresh their memory and maintain continuity. This shows that you value the relationship and have been attentive to their needs.
- **Multiple Communication Channels:** Vary your communication channels to reach your prospects where they are most active. In addition to LinkedIn messages, consider using email, phone calls, or even connecting on other social media platforms if appropriate.

Examples of Personalized Outreach and Follow-ups

To illustrate the effectiveness of personalized outreach and follow-ups, let's explore a couple of examples:

Example 1: Reconnecting with a Former Colleague:

"Hi [Colleague's Name], It's been a while since we last caught up, and I noticed on LinkedIn that you recently transitioned to a new role as a marketing director. Congratulations on the new position! I wanted to reconnect and see how things have been going for you. Given your expertise in digital marketing, I thought you might be interested in a new tool we've developed that can help streamline your marketing campaigns and improve ROI. I'd love to schedule a quick call to discuss it further. Let me know if you're available

next week. Looking forward to catching up!"

Example 2: Following up with a Prospect after a Networking Event:

"Hi [Prospect's Name], It was a pleasure meeting you at the industry conference yesterday. I enjoyed our conversation about the challenges your company is facing in customer retention. As promised, I've attached an e-book that provides in-depth strategies for improving customer loyalty. I believe you'll find it valuable. I'd be interested to hear your thoughts on the content and discuss how we can tailor those strategies to your specific business needs. If you're available for a call next week, please let me know. Thank you!"

Remember, the key to successful personalized outreach and follow-ups is to show genuine interest, provide value, and tailor your communication to the recipient's needs and interests. By employing these strategies and leveraging the power of personalization, you can build strong relationships that lead to long-term success on LinkedIn.

Providing Value through Content

Content is a powerful tool for nurturing relationships and establishing yourself as a trusted resource in your industry. By sharing valuable and relevant content, you provide continuous value to your connections and position yourself as an expert.

Curating and Sharing Industry Insights

Curate and share industry insights, trends, and news that are valuable to your target audience. This could include articles, reports, or thought leadership pieces. Add your unique perspective to the content you share, highlighting key takeaways or offering additional insights. By consistently providing valuable content, you demonstrate your expertise and deepen your connections' trust in your knowledge and capabilities. By consistently providing valuable and relevant information to your network, you can position yourself as a trusted source of expertise and deepen your connections with potential clients and partners. In this chapter, we will explore the importance of curating and sharing industry insights on LinkedIn and provide you with actionable strategies to effectively implement this approach.

The Value of Curating and Sharing Industry Insights

Curating and sharing industry insights serves multiple purposes in nurturing relationships on LinkedIn. Firstly, it demonstrates your knowledge and expertise in your field, allowing you to establish yourself as a credible authority. When you consistently share valuable content, your network will come to rely on you for industry updates, trends, and valuable insights.

Secondly, sharing industry insights helps to build trust and credibility with your connections. By consistently providing valuable information, you show that you are invested in the success of your network and genuinely interested in helping others. This can lead to increased engagement, meaningful conversations, and ultimately, long-term relationships.

Strategies for Effective Curating and Sharing

To curate and share industry insights effectively, consider the following strategies:

1. Identify Reliable Sources

It's crucial to curate content from reliable and authoritative sources within your industry. This could include reputable industry publications, research reports, influential thought leaders, or reputable blogs. By sharing content from trusted sources, you enhance your own credibility and ensure that the information you provide is accurate and valuable.

2. Focus on Relevance

When curating content, focus on selecting information that is relevant to your target audience. Consider their interests, pain points, and needs. Tailor the insights you share to address these specific areas, providing practical and actionable advice. This targeted approach will resonate with your connections and demonstrate your understanding of their industry challenges.

3. Add Value through Commentary

When sharing industry insights, don't simply repost or share links. Instead, add value by providing your own commentary and insights. Share your perspective on the information, highlight key takeaways, and offer practical tips or recommendations. This personal touch shows your expertise and adds depth to the content you share.

4. Encourage Engagement and Conversation

When sharing industry insights, aim to spark conversations and engage your network. Pose thought-provoking questions, ask for opinions, and encourage your connections to share their insights or experiences related to the content. Engage in meaningful discussions, respond to comments, and nurture the conversations that arise. This interactive approach fosters engagement and strengthens relationships.

Example: Curating and Sharing Industry Insights

Let's take a look at an example to illustrate the strategies discussed above.

Imagine you are a digital marketing expert focusing on content marketing. You come across an insightful article from a reputable marketing publication that discusses the latest trends in content distribution strategies.

Instead of simply sharing the article, you could apply the strategies mentioned earlier:

Title: The Future of Content Distribution: Emerging Trends and Strategies

Commentary: "Exciting insights on the future of content distribution! This article highlights the emerging trends that marketers need to pay attention to. I found the section on leveraging AI-driven algorithms particularly fascinating. It's clear that personalisation and targeting will play a significant role in the success of content distribution in the coming years. What are your thoughts on these trends? Are you already incorporating AI into your content distribution strategy?"

By adding your own commentary, posing questions, and inviting your network to share their thoughts, you create an engaging post that encourages conversation. This approach demonstrates your expertise, initiates meaningful interactions, and nurtures relationships with your connections. Remember, consistency is key when curating and sharing industry insights. Aim to provide valuable content on a regular basis, establish a reputation as a trusted source of information, and foster engagement within your network. By implementing these strategies, you can nurture relationships for long-term success on LinkedIn.

Creating Educational and Informative Content

Consider creating your own educational and informative content that addresses your connections' pain points and challenges. This could be in the form of blog posts, videos, infographics, or downloadable resources. Provide actionable advice, practical tips, and step-by-step guides that help your connections overcome their specific challenges. Educational content establishes you as a valuable resource and strengthens your relationships. Let's dive into the best practices and proven strategies for creating compelling educational content on LinkedIn.

Why Educational Content Matters

Educational content serves as a powerful tool for engaging your audience and establishing yourself as an authority in your industry. By sharing valuable insights, tips, and knowledge, you demonstrate your expertise and provide tangible value to your network. Educational content helps you build trust and credibility, making it easier to nurture relationships and convert leads into customers in the long run.

Identifying Relevant Topics

To create educational content that resonates with your audience, it's crucial to identify topics that are relevant and valuable to them. Consider the pain points, challenges, and questions your target audience commonly faces. Conduct research, listen to their feedback, and keep up with industry trends to stay informed about the topics that matter most to your network.

Providing Actionable Insights

When creating educational content, focus on providing actionable insights that your audience can implement and benefit from. Share practical tips, strategies, and step-by-step guides that empower your audience to take action and see results. By delivering tangible value, you position yourself as a trusted resource and increase the likelihood of engagement and conversion.

Formats for Educational Content

LinkedIn offers various formats to showcase your educational content. Consider these formats and choose the ones that align with your audience's preferences and the nature of your content:

1. **Articles and Blog Posts:** Write in-depth articles or blog posts that dive into a specific topic. Use storytelling techniques, data, and real-life examples to make your content engaging and relatable.
2. **Infographics:** Visualize complex information or data in an easy-to-understand and visually appealing format. Infographics are highly shareable and can grab the attention of your audience quickly.
3. **Videos:** Create informative and engaging videos where you share your knowledge and expertise. You can use screen recordings, interviews, or presentations to deliver your content effectively.

4. **Podcasts:** Host a podcast where you invite industry experts or share your insights on relevant topics. Podcasts provide a convenient way for your audience to consume educational content while on the go.

Citing Suitable Examples

Citing suitable examples in your educational content adds credibility and helps your audience better understand the concepts you're discussing.

Consider the following examples:
1. If you're writing an article about effective sales strategies, you can share a success story of how a company increased their sales by implementing a specific technique.
2. In a video discussing marketing trends, you can cite examples of

brands that successfully used innovative strategies to reach their target audience and achieve remarkable results.
3. When creating an infographic about productivity hacks, you can include real-life examples of individuals or businesses that improved their productivity by adopting specific practices.

By incorporating relevant and relatable examples, you make your educational content more engaging and impactful, increasing the chances of resonating with your audience.

Building Communities and Networking

LinkedIn offers various opportunities to build communities and expand your network. By actively participating in groups, events, and conversations, you can connect with like-minded professionals, engage with your target audience, and foster valuable relationships.

Joining and Contributing to Groups

Identify and join LinkedIn groups that align with your industry or target audience. Actively contribute by sharing insights, answering questions, and participating in discussions. Be a helpful resource and provide value to other group members. Engage with group leaders and influencers, and build relationships with fellow professionals who can become potential clients, partners, or advocates for your brand.

Networking through Events and Webinars

Take advantage of LinkedIn's events and webinars to expand your network and establish new relationships. Attend relevant events and engage with participants through meaningful conversations and connections. Consider hosting your own webinars or virtual events to share your expertise and attract interested prospects. Networking through events creates opportunities to nurture relationships and uncover new business prospects.

Leveraging LinkedIn Sales Navigator

LinkedIn Sales Navigator is a powerful tool that can enhance your relationship-building efforts. It provides advanced search filters, lead recommendations, and real-time insights to help you identify and engage with your target audience effectively. In this section, we will delve into the strategies and features of LinkedIn Sales Navigator that can help you build and nurture relationships effectively.

What is LinkedIn Sales Navigator?

LinkedIn Sales Navigator is a premium tool designed specifically for sales professionals. It offers a range of features and functionalities that enable targeted prospecting, lead nurturing, and relationship building. With Sales Navigator, you can access valuable insights, expand your network, and engage with prospects in a more personalised and meaningful way.

Strategies for Leveraging LinkedIn Sales Navigator

1. Advanced Search and Filtering:

LinkedIn Sales Navigator provides robust search and filtering options, allowing you to identify your ideal prospects based on various criteria. Here are some strategies to effectively leverage this feature:

- **Targeted Industry and Job Titles:** Use the advanced search filters to narrow down your search based on the industry and specific job titles relevant to your target audience. For example, if you offer marketing consultancy services, you can search for Marketing Managers or Chief Marketing Officers within the industries you specialize in.

- **Geographic Focus:** Refine your search by location to connect with prospects in specific regions or countries. This is particularly useful if your products or services cater to a specific geographic market.

2. Saved Leads and Alerts:

LinkedIn Sales Navigator allows you to save leads and receive real-time alerts, keeping you updated on their activities and enabling timely engagement. Here are some strategies to make the most of this feature:

- **Strategic Monitoring:** Save leads that align with your target customer profile and regularly review the alerts to stay informed about their updates, such as job changes, company news, or content they share. This provides valuable insights for initiating conversations and nurturing relationships.

- **Engaging with Relevant Updates:** When you receive an alert about a lead's activity, such as publishing an article or sharing a post, take the opportunity to engage with their content. Leave thoughtful comments or share their content within your network, showcasing your interest and expertise. This helps build rapport and increases the chances of starting a meaningful conversation.

3. **InMail and Personalized Messaging:**

InMail allows you to send direct messages to prospects who are not in your network. Personalised messaging is key to establishing meaningful connections. Here are some strategies to leverage InMail effectively:

- **Research and Personalisation:** Before reaching out, thoroughly research the prospect's background, interests, and recent activities. Use this information to tailor your message and show that you have taken the time to understand their needs. For example, you can reference a recent industry event they attended or an article they published and express your interest in discussing related topics.
- **Value-Oriented Approach:** Focus on providing value in your InMail messages. Highlight how your product or service can solve a specific challenge they may be facing. Share relevant insights, case studies, or success stories to

demonstrate the benefits they can expect from working with you.

Examples of Leveraging LinkedIn Sales Navigator

- **Example 1:** Imagine you are a sales professional offering **HR consulting services.** By using LinkedIn Sales Navigator, you can search for HR Directors in the manufacturing industry within a 50-mile radius of your location. You can further narrow down the search by filtering for companies with more than 500 employees. This targeted approach allows you to connect with prospects who are likely to have HR challenges and a higher potential for requiring your expertise.
- **Example 2:** Suppose you are a sales representative for a software

company specializing in customer relationship management (**CRM**) solutions. You receive an alert from LinkedIn Sales Navigator that one of your saved leads, a Sales Manager at a large tech company, has shared an article about improving sales productivity. You take this opportunity to engage with their post by leaving a comment expressing your appreciation for the insights shared and sharing the article with your network. This interaction helps initiate a conversation and positions you as a knowledgeable resource in the field.

Summary

Chapter 3 of "LinkedIn Sales Mastery: Unlocking Profitable Leads and

Dominating the Global Market" emphasises the significance of nurturing relationships for long-term success on LinkedIn. By employing the strategies outlined in this chapter, such as active listening and engagement, personalized outreach, providing value through content, building communities, and leveraging LinkedIn Sales Navigator, you can develop strong and meaningful connections that lead to lasting business relationships and enable you to dominate the global market.

Chapter 4: Leveraging LinkedIn Groups for Targeted Engagement

In this chapter, we dive into the power of LinkedIn Groups as a valuable tool for targeted engagement. LinkedIn Groups provide a unique opportunity to connect with like-minded professionals, share insights, and build relationships within specific industries or interest areas. We will explore proven strategies to effectively leverage LinkedIn Groups to unlock profitable leads and dominate the global market.

Understanding the Benefits of LinkedIn Groups

LinkedIn Groups offer several benefits that make them an essential component of your sales and networking strategy. By joining and actively engaging in relevant groups, you can:

Connect with Targeted Audiences

LinkedIn Groups provide access to a highly targeted audience of professionals who share common interests or work in specific industries. This allows you to connect with individuals who are more likely to be interested in your products or services. Engaging with a niche audience in groups increases the chances of generating quality leads and building meaningful relationships.

Establish Authority and Credibility

Actively participating in LinkedIn Groups allows you to showcase your expertise and establish yourself as a thought leader in your industry. By sharing valuable insights, answering questions, and providing helpful resources, you can position yourself as a trusted authority. Building credibility within groups enhances your reputation and attracts potential clients or collaborators who value your expertise.

Identifying and Joining Relevant Groups

To effectively leverage LinkedIn Groups, it's essential to identify and join groups that align with your target audience and industry. Here are some strategies to find and join relevant groups:

Research and Explore

Conduct thorough research on LinkedIn to identify groups that cater to your target market. Search for groups using relevant keywords, industry-specific terms, or job titles. Explore the groups' descriptions, discussions, and member profiles to ensure they align with your objectives and provide opportunities for meaningful engagement.

Evaluate Group Activity and Engagement

Assess the activity level and engagement within a group before joining. Look for groups with regular discussions, active participation, and a healthy number of members. Avoid groups with low engagement or a high number of spam posts. A vibrant and engaged community is more likely to provide valuable networking opportunities and potential leads.

Engaging and Adding Value

Once you've joined relevant LinkedIn Groups, it's crucial to engage actively and provide value to the community. Here are some effective strategies to maximise your engagement:

Participate in Discussions

Engage in group discussions by sharing your insights, expertise, and perspectives on relevant topics. Offer thoughtful comments and ask insightful questions that spark meaningful conversations. Actively contribute to discussions to establish yourself as a valuable member of the community and attract the attention of potential leads.

Share Valuable Resources

Share relevant and valuable resources such as articles, blog posts, reports, or case studies within the group. Ensure that the content you share provides actionable insights or solves common pain points for the group members. Sharing valuable resources positions you as a helpful resource and encourages others to engage with you.

Building Relationships

LinkedIn Groups provide an excellent opportunity to build relationships with individuals who share common interests or work in similar industries. Here are strategies to foster meaningful connections:

Connect with Group Members

Identify individuals within the group who are active and share valuable insights. Send them personalised connection requests, mentioning your mutual interest in the group and expressing your desire to connect and collaborate. Building connections with active and engaged group members increases your chances of nurturing valuable relationships.

Initiate Private Conversations

LinkedIn Groups offer the option to send private messages to other members. Utilise this feature to initiate private conversations with individuals who have expressed interest in your posts or have valuable insights to offer. Engage in meaningful discussions, share resources, and explore potential collaboration opportunities.

Summary

Chapter 4 of "LinkedIn Sales Mastery: Unlocking Profitable Leads and Dominating the Global Market" highlights the significance of leveraging LinkedIn Groups for targeted engagement. By understanding the benefits of LinkedIn Groups, joining relevant groups, actively engaging, providing value, and building relationships within the groups, you can unlock profitable leads and establish yourself as an authority in your industry. By implementing the strategies outlined in this chapter, you will be well-equipped to leverage LinkedIn Groups to their full potential and gain a competitive edge in the global market.

Chapter 5: Mastering LinkedIn Sales Navigator

In this chapter, we delve into the powerful features and strategies of LinkedIn Sales Navigator. LinkedIn Sales Navigator is a premium tool designed specifically for sales professionals to unlock profitable leads and dominate the global market. We will explore the functionalities and proven strategies to master LinkedIn Sales Navigator and elevate your sales efforts to new heights.

Understanding the Benefits of LinkedIn Sales Navigator

LinkedIn Sales Navigator provides a range of benefits that can significantly enhance your sales effectiveness. By mastering this tool, you can:

Identify and Target the Right Prospects

LinkedIn Sales Navigator offers advanced search filters that allow you to identify and target prospects based on specific criteria. Narrow down your search by industry, job title, company size, location, and more. This precision targeting enables you to focus your efforts on high-potential leads, increasing the likelihood of generating profitable opportunities.

Access Real-time Insights

Stay informed about your prospects and connections with real-time insights. LinkedIn Sales Navigator provides valuable information, such as job changes, company updates, and engagement activities. Utilize these insights to personalize your outreach and engage with prospects based on their current circumstances. Real-time insights give you a competitive edge and help you tailor your approach for maximum impact.

Harnessing Advanced Search and Lead Recommendations

LinkedIn Sales Navigator offers powerful search capabilities and leads recommendations to support your sales efforts. Here's how you can make the most of these features:

Utilize Advanced Search Filters

Take advantage of Sales Navigator's advanced search filters to refine your prospecting efforts. Utilize the various criteria to target specific industries, job functions, seniority levels, and more. By narrowing down your search, you can focus on prospects who are most likely to be interested in your offerings and have the authority to make purchasing decisions.

Leverage Lead Recommendations

Sales Navigator provides lead recommendations based on your saved leads, connections, and search history. These recommendations offer valuable insights into potential prospects who align with your target audience. Explore these recommendations to discover new opportunities for relationship building and sales growth. Actively engaging with these recommended leads can lead to valuable connections and lucrative business opportunities.

Engaging with Personalized Outreach and InMail Messages

LinkedIn Sales Navigator offers InMail messages, a powerful feature that allows you to send direct messages to prospects even if you're not connected. Here's how you can leverage personalized outreach and InMail messages effectively:

Craft Personalized Outreach Messages

When reaching out to prospects, personalization is key. Tailor your messages to address their specific pain points, challenges, or interests. Show that you have done your research and understand their industry or role. By demonstrating a genuine interest in their success and offering tailored solutions, you significantly increase the chances of capturing their attention and initiating meaningful conversations.

Utilize InMail Messages Strategically

InMail messages provide a direct line of communication with prospects, giving you the opportunity to make a compelling pitch or offer. However, it's important to use InMail messages strategically and avoid being overly sales-driven or intrusive. Craft engaging and concise messages that clearly communicate the value you can provide. Personalize your InMail messages by referencing shared connections, group memberships, or common interests to establish rapport and credibility.

Tracking and Measuring Success

LinkedIn Sales Navigator offers robust tracking and measurement capabilities that enable you to assess the effectiveness of your sales efforts. Here's how you can make use of these features:

Monitor Account and Lead Activity

Keep track of account and lead activities using Sales Navigator's tracking features. Monitor profile views, post engagement, and interactions with your content. This information provides insights into the level of interest and engagement of your prospects. Use these metrics to prioritize follow-ups, identify warm leads, and gauge the effectiveness of your outreach strategies.

Utilize TeamLink and Team Reporting

If you're part of a sales team, leverage TeamLink and Team Reporting features in Sales Navigator. TeamLink allows you to see who within your organization has connections with prospects, increasing your chances of securing warm introductions. Team Reporting provides visibility into the collective sales efforts, allowing you to identify best practices, measure team performance, and align strategies for optimal results.

Summary

Chapter 5 of "LinkedIn Sales Mastery: Unlocking Profitable Leads and Dominating the Global Market" focuses on mastering LinkedIn Sales Navigator to enhance your sales effectiveness. By understanding the benefits of Sales Navigator, harnessing advanced search filters and lead recommendations, engaging in personalized outreach, utilizing InMail messages strategically, and tracking your success, you can leverage this powerful tool to unlock profitable leads and gain a competitive advantage in the global market.

Chapter 6: Creating Compelling Content for LinkedIn

In this chapter, we explore the art of creating compelling content on LinkedIn to attract and engage your target audience. Content plays a crucial role in establishing your credibility, building relationships, and ultimately unlocking profitable leads. We will delve into proven strategies and best practices for creating captivating content that resonates with your audience and helps you dominate the global market.

Understanding the Importance of Compelling Content

Compelling content is crucial for building credibility, establishing thought leadership, and driving meaningful interactions with your network. In this section, we will discuss the strategies and examples that can help you understand the importance of creating compelling content on LinkedIn.

Why is Compelling Content Important?

Compelling content is the key to capturing the attention and interest of your target audience on LinkedIn. It enables you to establish yourself as an authority in your industry and differentiate yourself from competitors. When you consistently produce valuable and engaging content, you build trust and credibility among your connections, which can ultimately lead to new opportunities and business growth.

Strategies for Creating Compelling Content

1. Know Your Audience

To create compelling content, you must have a deep understanding of your target audience. Research their needs, pain points, and interests. Consider the challenges they face and the information they seek. By knowing your audience, you can tailor your content to resonate with their specific needs and preferences.

2. Provide Valuable Insights

Compelling content should provide value to your audience. Share industry insights, tips, best practices, and actionable advice. Help your audience solve problems, overcome challenges, and achieve their goals. When you consistently deliver valuable content, you position yourself as a trusted resource, and people will actively seek out your expertise.

For example, if you are a **digital marketing consultant,** you can create content that explains the latest trends and strategies in the industry. Share practical tips on **improving SEO**, **increasing conversion rates**, or **optimizing social media campaigns.** By offering valuable insights, you establish yourself as an authority and attract a following of engaged professionals seeking your expertise.

3. Utilize Visual Elements

Visual elements play a crucial role in capturing attention and increasing engagement on LinkedIn. Incorporate eye-catching images, videos, infographics, and SlideShare presentations into your content. Visual content tends to grab more attention in busy newsfeeds and helps communicate information in a more engaging and memorable way.

For instance, if you are sharing statistics or data, present them in a visually appealing infographic or create a short video summarizing key points. Visual content not only enhances the visual appeal but also improves comprehension and shareability, increasing the reach and impact of your message.

Examples of Compelling Content

1. Thought Leadership Articles

Write thought-provoking articles on LinkedIn's publishing platform. Share your unique perspectives, industry insights, and actionable advice. Provide in-depth analysis and offer solutions to common industry challenges. Thought leadership articles demonstrate your expertise and position you as a trusted industry influencer.

For instance, a human resources consultant could write an article on "**5 Strategies for Building a High-Performing Remote Team**" or a cybersecurity expert could share insights on "**Emerging Cybersecurity Threats and How to Mitigate Them.**" By showcasing your knowledge and expertise, you attract a relevant and engaged audience.

2. Engaging Visual Content

Create visually appealing and informative content that stands out in the newsfeed. Share infographics, SlideShare presentations, or videos that convey valuable information in a visually appealing manner. Visual content is highly shareable and can help increase your reach and engagement.

For example, a **social media marketer** could create an infographic showcasing "*10 Strategies for Driving Engagement on Instagram" or a sales trainer could create a SlideShare presentation on "Effective Negotiation Techniques for Sales Professionals.*" These visual assets are not only informative but also visually compelling, making them more likely to be shared and engaged with by your network.

3. Interactive Polls and Surveys

Engage your audience by creating polls or surveys related to your industry or a specific topic. This encourages participation and generates valuable insights. Use the results to create follow-up content that addresses the interests and preferences of your audience.

For instance, a **marketing consultant** could create a poll asking, "*What is your biggest content marketing challenge?*" or a career coach could conduct a survey on "*Top Skills Employers Look for in 2023.*" By involving your audience, you not only gather valuable data but also show that you value their opinions and are committed to addressing their needs.

Compelling content is the cornerstone of your LinkedIn presence. It enables you to:

Establish Authority and Thought Leadership

By consistently sharing valuable and insightful content, you position yourself as an authority in your industry. Your content should showcase your expertise, provide unique perspectives, and address the pain points and challenges faced by your target audience. By establishing yourself as a thought leader, you gain credibility and attract the attention of potential clients and collaborators.

Build Relationships and Trust

Compelling content fosters meaningful connections by offering value to your audience. When your content consistently delivers valuable insights, solutions, and inspiration, it builds trust and loyalty among your followers. This trust lays the foundation for long-term relationships that can lead to profitable business opportunities.

Identifying Your Target Audience and Understanding Their Needs

Before creating content, it's crucial to identify your target audience and understand their needs, preferences, and pain points. Here's how you can do it:

Conduct Market Research

Research your industry, niche, and target market to gain a deeper understanding of your audience. Identify their demographics, interests, challenges, and aspirations. Use tools like LinkedIn Insights and Google Analytics to gather data and insights about your audience's preferences and behaviour.

Create Buyer Personas

Develop detailed buyer personas that represent your ideal customers. Consider their job titles, responsibilities, goals, and challenges. Understand their motivations and pain points, and tailor your content to address these specific needs. Creating buyer personas helps you create targeted and relevant content that resonates with your audience.

Crafting Engaging and Valuable Content

To create compelling content that captivates your audience, consider the following strategies:

Choose Relevant Topics

Select topics that are relevant to your industry, target audience, and current trends. Stay updated with the latest news, developments, and challenges in your field. Your content should provide valuable insights, practical tips, and solutions that your audience can apply to their professional lives.

Utilize Different Content Formats

Diversify your content formats to cater to different preferences and consumption habits. Consider using a mix of articles, videos, infographics, podcasts, and SlideShare presentations. Experiment with various formats to see which ones resonate most with your audience.

Craft Attention-Grabbing Headlines

A compelling headline is crucial for capturing your audience's attention. Use powerful, descriptive, and curiosity-inducing headlines that compel people to click and read your content. Incorporate keywords relevant to your topic and make the value proposition clear from the start.

Provide Actionable Insights and Solutions

Your content should provide actionable insights, practical tips, and solutions that your audience can apply in their professional lives. Make your content informative, educational, and actionable to demonstrate your expertise and provide genuine value to your audience.

Leverage Visuals and Multimedia

Visuals can significantly enhance the appeal and impact of your content. Incorporate high-quality images, charts, and graphs to support your key points and make your content visually engaging. Consider using videos, animations, and interactive elements to create more dynamic and immersive content experiences.

Engaging with Your Audience and Encouraging Interaction

Engagement is key to the success of your content strategy on LinkedIn. Here are strategies to actively engage with your audience:

Respond to Comments and Messages

When people comment on your posts or send you messages, respond promptly and thoughtfully. Engage in conversations, answer questions, and show genuine interest in their thoughts and opinions. This two-way interaction strengthens relationships and establishes you as an approachable and responsive professional.

Participate in LinkedIn Groups

Join relevant LinkedIn Groups in your industry and actively participate in discussions. Share your insights, contribute valuable information, and offer guidance to group members. Engaging in group conversations expands your reach, increases your visibility, and helps you build relationships with like-minded professionals.

Measuring and Refining Your Content Strategy

To ensure the effectiveness of your content strategy, measure key metrics and make data-driven refinements:

Analyze Post Performance

Track the performance of your posts using LinkedIn's analytics tools. Analyze metrics such as views, likes, comments, and shares to understand what resonates with your audience. Identify the types of content, topics, and formats that generate the most engagement, and replicate their success in future posts. Now we will discuss strategies and techniques for analysing post performance on LinkedIn and refining your content strategy for optimal results.

Measuring Post Performance on LinkedIn

LinkedIn provides valuable analytics and insights that can help you evaluate the effectiveness of your content. By understanding how your posts perform, you can identify what resonates with your audience and make informed decisions to enhance your content strategy.

Here are some key strategies and metrics to consider:

1. **Engagement Metrics:** LinkedIn provides metrics such as likes, comments, and shares that indicate how well your audience is engaging with your content. Pay attention to the number of likes, as it reflects the

initial interest generated by your post. Comments provide insights into the level of conversation and discussions sparked by your content. Shares indicate the willingness of your audience to amplify your message within their networks. By monitoring these engagement metrics, you can assess the overall impact and relevance of your content.

Example Strategy: Analyse your most engaging posts and identify common themes, topics, or formats that receive high levels of interaction. For instance, if you notice that your audience engages more with posts that feature practical tips or industry insights, you can focus on creating more content of a similar nature to drive further engagement.

2. **Reach and Impressions:** LinkedIn also provides data on the reach and impressions of your posts. Reach refers to the number of unique individuals who have seen your content, while impressions indicate the total number of times your content has been displayed. By tracking these metrics, you can assess the visibility and impact of your posts among your target audience.

   Example Strategy: Compare the reach and impressions of your different types of content. If you find that certain formats or topics consistently generate higher reach and impressions, consider incorporating more of these elements into your content strategy. Additionally, analyse the demographics and industries of the audience reached to ensure alignment with your target market.

3. **Click-through Rates:** LinkedIn enables you to track the click-through rates (CTR) of your posts, indicating the percentage of users who clicked on a link or CTA within your content. Monitoring CTR helps evaluate the effectiveness of your call-to-action and the level of interest your audience has in exploring further.
Example Strategy: Analyse posts with high CTRs and assess the elements that contribute to their success. It could be a compelling headline, a clear and enticing CTA, or the inclusion of multimedia content. Incorporate these elements into future posts to drive higher click-through rates and guide your

audience towards your desired actions.

Refining Your Content Strategy

Once you have gathered data on your post performance, it's essential to refine your content strategy accordingly. Here are some strategies and approaches to consider:

1. **Content Themes and Topics:** Analyse the performance of different content themes and topics to identify the ones that resonate most with your audience. Focus on creating content that aligns with their interests and pain points, offering valuable insights or solutions.
   Example Strategy: Suppose you notice that your audience engages more with posts related to career development or productivity tips. In

that case, you can dedicate more of your content to these topics and position yourself as an expert in those areas.

2. **Content Formats:** Experiment with different content formats, such as text-based posts, images, videos, or infographics, to determine which formats generate the most engagement and reach.

   Example Strategy: If you find that videos consistently receive higher engagement and reach compared to other formats, consider incorporating more video content into your strategy. Experiment with different video types, such as tutorials, interviews, or industry insights, to keep your content varied and engaging.

3. **Optimize Headlines and CTAs:** Pay attention to the performance of your headlines and calls-to-action (CTAs). Refine and test different variations to capture your audience's attention and encourage them to take action.
   Example Strategy: If you discover that headlines with numbers or intriguing questions generate more clicks, incorporate these elements into your future posts. Similarly, experiment with different CTAs to find the ones that drive the desired actions, such as downloading a resource or signing up for a webinar.
4. **Consistency and Timing:** Analyse the best days and times for posting to maximise visibility and engagement. Consistency in posting helps establish a reliable presence

and ensures your audience knows when to expect new content.

Example Strategy: If you find that your audience engages more during weekday mornings, schedule your posts accordingly to increase visibility and interactions. Test different posting times to identify the optimal time slots for your specific audience.

By regularly measuring and refining your content strategy based on data-driven insights, you can continuously improve your LinkedIn content and achieve greater engagement and long-term success.

A/B Test and Experiment

Continuously test and experiment with different content strategies to optimize your results. Try varying post formats, headlines, visuals, and messaging to gauge their impact on engagement and conversions. Use A/B testing to compare different variations and refine your approach based on the data. In this section, we will explore the strategy of A/B testing and experimenting to measure and refine your content strategy on LinkedIn.

Why A/B Test and Experiment?

A/B testing is a powerful method that allows you to compare two different versions of a piece of content and measure which one performs better in terms of engagement, click-through rates, conversions, and other key metrics. By conducting experiments and analysing the results, you can gain valuable insights into what resonates with your audience and make data-driven decisions to refine your content strategy.

A/B Testing Strategies on LinkedIn

1. **Headlines and Post Formats:** Experiment with different headline styles and post formats to see which ones attract more clicks and engagement. For example, you can test using question-based headlines versus informative headlines or try sharing your content as a text post, image post, or video post. By tracking the performance of each variation, you can determine which formats generate the most interest from your target audience.
   Example: A marketing agency could A/B test two headlines for a blog post on LinkedIn. Headline A could be *"10

Proven Marketing Strategies for Boosting Your Online Presence," while Headline B could be *"Are You Making These Common Marketing Mistakes? Find Out Now!"* By comparing the click-through rates and engagement metrics of both headlines, they can identify which one grabs more attention and generates higher engagement.

2. **Visual Elements:** Test different visual elements, such as images, infographics, or videos, to determine which ones resonate best with your audience. Experiment with different designs, colours, and compositions to find the visuals that enhance the impact of your content.

   Example: An e-commerce brand could A/B test product images with plain backgrounds versus lifestyle images featuring their products being used in real-life scenarios. By monitoring the click-through rates and conversion rates associated with each variation, they can understand which visual style is more persuasive in driving customer interest and purchases.

Measurement and Refinement

To effectively measure and refine your content strategy, consider the following strategies:

1. **Identify Key Metrics:** Determine the key metrics you want to track, such as click-through rates, engagement levels, conversion rates, or time spent on the page. Select metrics that align with your content goals and help you evaluate the success of your experiments.

2. **Split Your Audience:** Divide your target audience into smaller segments and expose each segment to different content variations. This allows you to compare the performance of each variation within a controlled environment.
3. **Analyse Results:** Analyse the performance data of each variation and compare the results. Look for patterns and trends that indicate which content elements resonate best with your audience. Identify the winning variation and use those insights to refine your future content strategy.
4. **Iterate and Optimise:** Based on the insights gained from A/B testing and experimentation, iterate and optimise your content strategy. Implement the learnings from

successful variations and continually refine your approach to maximise engagement and achieve your goals. By conducting A/B tests and experiments, you can gain a deeper understanding of your audience's preferences and refine your content strategy accordingly. Remember to track the results, analyse the data, and continuously iterate to create compelling content that drives engagement and generates profitable leads on LinkedIn.

Summary

Chapter 6 of "LinkedIn Sales Mastery: Unlocking Profitable Leads and Dominating the Global Market" focuses on creating compelling content on LinkedIn to attract, engage, and convert your target audience. By understanding the importance of compelling content, identifying your target audience's needs, crafting engaging content, encouraging interaction, and measuring your content strategy, you can establish your authority, build relationships, and unlock profitable leads on the platform.

Chapter 7: Maximizing LinkedIn Advertising Opportunities

In this chapter, we explore the powerful advertising opportunities available on LinkedIn and how you can leverage them to unlock profitable leads and dominate the global market. LinkedIn's advertising platform provides a targeted and effective way to reach your ideal audience and drive meaningful engagement. We will dive into proven strategies and best practices to maximize the impact of your LinkedIn advertising campaigns.

Understanding the Benefits of LinkedIn Advertising

LinkedIn advertising offers several unique benefits that make it a valuable tool for your sales and marketing efforts. By utilizing LinkedIn's advertising opportunities, you can:

Reach a Highly Targeted Audience

LinkedIn provides advanced targeting options that allow you to reach your desired audience with precision. You can target based on factors such as job title, industry, company size, seniority, and more. This level of granularity ensures that your ads are shown to the individuals who are most likely to be interested in your products or services, increasing the chances of generating profitable leads.

Leverage Professional Data and Insights

LinkedIn has a wealth of professional data that can be used to refine your advertising campaigns. You can tap into insights about your target audience's professional backgrounds, skills, interests, and behaviours. This data enables you to tailor your messaging and creative elements to resonate with your audience and drive higher engagement.

Choosing the Right Advertising Objectives

When creating LinkedIn ad campaigns, it's essential to choose the right advertising objectives based on your sales goals. Here are some common objectives and how they can contribute to your success:

Lead Generation

If your primary goal is to generate leads, you can create lead generation campaigns on LinkedIn. These campaigns include lead gen forms that allow users to submit their contact information directly within the ad, making it easy for prospects to express interest in your offerings. By utilizing lead gen forms, you can capture high-quality leads and nurture them towards conversion.

Brand Awareness

If your focus is on increasing brand visibility and awareness, consider brand awareness campaigns. These campaigns aim to reach a broad audience and generate impressions. They help you increase brand recall, establish familiarity, and create a positive brand image among your target audience.

Website Traffic

To drive traffic to your website and increase conversions, utilize website traffic campaigns. These campaigns direct users to specific landing pages or content on your website. By leveraging LinkedIn's precise targeting capabilities, you can drive relevant traffic to your site, increasing the chances of capturing leads or driving desired actions.

Strategies for Driving Website Traffic through LinkedIn

To maximise your LinkedIn advertising efforts and generate website traffic, consider implementing the following strategies:

1. Sponsored Content

Sponsored Content is an effective way to promote your website and drive traffic. You can create compelling and informative posts that provide value to your target audience. These posts can include a call-to-action (CTA) with a link to your website, encouraging users to visit and learn more about your offerings.

Example:

Suppose you run a digital marketing agency. You can create a sponsored content post that offers tips and insights on improving SEO. At the end of the post, include a CTA to visit your website for a comprehensive SEO guide. This strategy entices LinkedIn users to click on the link and visit your website for more valuable information.

2. Text Ads

LinkedIn Text Ads are another effective way to drive traffic to your website. These ads appear on the LinkedIn platform and allow you to create concise and engaging messages with a link to your website. Use compelling copy and a clear CTA to entice users to click and visit your website.

Example:

Suppose you have an **e-commerce website** selling sustainable fashion products. You can create a Text Ad that highlights your latest collection and offers a discount code. The ad can include a CTA to visit your website and use the discount code at checkout. This strategy encourages LinkedIn users to click on the ad and browse your website to make a purchase.

3. Showcase Pages

LinkedIn Showcase Pages allow you to create dedicated pages for specific **products**, **services**, or **campaigns**. These pages can be customized with unique content and visuals, providing an opportunity to showcase your offerings and drive traffic to your website.

Example:

Suppose you have a **software company** with multiple products. Create a Showcase Page for each product, highlighting its features and benefits. Include links on each Showcase Page that direct users to the corresponding product page on your website. This strategy not only increases website traffic but also provides a focused and tailored experience for users interested in specific products.

4. Sponsored InMail

Sponsored InMail allows you to send personalized messages to LinkedIn users directly in their inboxes. Use this feature to send targeted messages with a CTA that directs recipients to your website. Personalize the messages based on the recipient's profile information and their interests to increase engagement and click-through rates.

Example:

Suppose you offer a professional coaching program. Use Sponsored InMail to send personalized messages to LinkedIn users who match your target audience criteria, such as recent graduates or professionals seeking career advancement. In the message, provide information about your coaching program and include a CTA to visit your website for more details. This strategy drives website traffic by capturing the attention of your target audience and directing them to your website for further information.

Designing Compelling Advertisements

To maximize the impact of your LinkedIn advertising campaigns, it's crucial to design compelling advertisements. Here are some strategies to create attention-grabbing ads:

Clear and Concise Messaging

Craft your ad copy to be clear, concise, and compelling. Clearly communicate the value proposition of your product or service and how it can benefit the audience. Use concise and impactful language to capture attention and entice users to engage further.

Engaging Visuals

Utilize visually appealing images or videos that align with your brand and capture the attention of your target audience. High-quality visuals can help your ad stand out and effectively convey your message. Consider using images of people or relevant scenes that resonate with your audience's professional aspirations and goals.

Call-to-Action (CTA)

Include a strong and clear call-to-action in your ads. Guide users on the action you want them to take, such as "**Sign up now,**" "**Learn more,**" or "**Request a demo.**" The CTA should be compelling and aligned with your advertising objective.

Optimizing and Monitoring Your Campaigns

To ensure the success of your LinkedIn advertising campaigns, it's important to optimize and monitor them continuously. Here's how you can do it:

Monitoring and Adjusting

Regularly monitor the performance of your campaigns using LinkedIn's advertising analytics. Pay attention to key metrics such as click-through rates (CTR), conversion rates, and cost-per-acquisition (CPA). If certain campaigns or ads are underperforming, adjust your targeting, messaging, or creative elements to improve their effectiveness.

Summary

Chapter 7 of "LinkedIn Sales Mastery: Unlocking Profitable Leads and Dominating the Global Market" focuses on maximizing LinkedIn advertising opportunities to drive profitable leads and achieve dominance in the global market. By understanding the benefits of LinkedIn advertising, choosing the right objectives, designing compelling advertisements, and optimizing your campaigns, you can effectively reach your target audience, increase brand visibility, and generate valuable leads.

Chapter 8: Harnessing LinkedIn Analytics for Data-Driven Success

In this chapter, we delve into the power of LinkedIn analytics and how it can be leveraged to drive data-driven success in your sales and marketing efforts. LinkedIn provides a wealth of valuable insights and metrics that can help you understand the performance of your activities, identify opportunities for improvement, and make informed decisions to unlock profitable leads and dominate the global market. We will explore proven strategies and best practices for harnessing LinkedIn analytics effectively.

The Importance of LinkedIn Analytics

LinkedIn analytics empowers you with actionable data and insights to measure the impact of your LinkedIn activities and drive success. By harnessing LinkedIn analytics, you can:

Measure Performance and Effectiveness

LinkedIn analytics allows you to track key metrics and understand how your posts, campaigns, and profile are performing. It provides valuable insights into metrics such as impressions, engagement, click-through rates (CTR), follower growth, and more. Monitoring these metrics helps you gauge the effectiveness of your strategies and make data-driven improvements.

Understand Your Audience

LinkedIn analytics provides detailed information about your audience demographics, interests, and engagement patterns. By understanding your audience better, you can tailor your content, messaging, and targeting to resonate with their preferences and needs. This deeper understanding enables you to create more relevant and impactful campaigns.

Key Metrics and Measurements to Focus On

To drive data-driven success on LinkedIn, it's important to focus on key metrics and measurements. Here are some metrics you should pay attention to:

Impressions and Reach

Impressions indicate the number of times your content or ads have been displayed to users. Reach represents the unique number of users who have seen your content. Monitoring impressions and reach helps you understand the visibility and reach of your LinkedIn activities.

Engagement Metrics

Engagement metrics, such as likes, comments, shares, and click-through rates (CTR), provide insights into the level of interaction and interest your content generates. Higher engagement indicates that your content resonates with your audience and encourages them to take action.

Follower Growth

Tracking your follower growth allows you to understand how your audience is expanding over time. A growing follower base signifies that your content is attracting attention and generating interest. Monitor follower growth to gauge the effectiveness of your content strategy and identify trends.

Conversion Metrics

If you have specific conversion goals, such as lead generation or website traffic, monitor conversion metrics. These metrics include click-throughs to your website, form submissions, or other desired actions. By tracking conversions, you can assess the effectiveness of your LinkedIn activities in driving tangible business outcomes.

Using Analytics to Refine Your Strategy

LinkedIn analytics provides valuable insights that can inform and refine your sales and marketing strategy. Here's how you can use analytics to drive success:

Identify High-Performing Content

Analyzing the performance of your content allows you to identify what resonates most with your audience. Look for patterns and trends in your top-performing posts or campaigns. Identify the content types, topics, formats, and messaging that generate the highest engagement and replicate their success in future content.

Optimize Posting Times

LinkedIn analytics can help you determine the most effective times to post your content. Identify the time periods when your audience is most active and engaged. By strategically scheduling your posts during these peak times, you can maximize visibility, reach, and engagement.

Refine Targeting and Segmentation

By analysing audience demographics and engagement data, you can refine your targeting and segmentation strategies. Identify the segments that show the highest engagement and conversion rates. Tailor your messaging and targeting parameters to effectively reach these high-performing segments.

Track Competitor Performance

LinkedIn analytics also allows you to monitor your competitors' performance. Analyze their content, engagement metrics, and follower growth to gain insights into their strategies. Identify areas where you can differentiate yourself and learn from their successes and failures.

Summary

Chapter 8 of "LinkedIn Sales Mastery: Unlocking Profitable Leads and Dominating the Global Market" focuses on harnessing LinkedIn analytics for data-driven success. By understanding the importance of LinkedIn analytics, focusing on key metrics, utilizing analytics to refine your strategy, and leveraging insights to make informed decisions, you can unlock profitable leads and dominate the global market on LinkedIn.

Chapter 9: Expanding Your Reach with LinkedIn Influencers

In this chapter, we explore the power of LinkedIn influencers and how you can leverage their influence to expand your reach, build credibility, and unlock profitable leads. LinkedIn influencers are industry leaders, experts, and thought influencers who have a significant following and engage with a wide audience. By strategically partnering with influencers on LinkedIn, you can tap into their network, gain visibility, and dominate the global market. We will discuss proven strategies and best practices for effectively collaborating with LinkedIn influencers.

The Benefits of Partnering with LinkedIn Influencers

Partnering with LinkedIn influencers offers several benefits that can accelerate your sales and marketing efforts. Here are some key advantages:

Increased Visibility and Reach

LinkedIn influencers have a substantial following and a dedicated audience that trusts their expertise. By collaborating with influencers, you gain access to their network, expanding your reach to a broader and more relevant audience. This increased visibility can significantly enhance your brand awareness and attract potential customers.

Enhanced Credibility and Trust

Influencers have established themselves as trusted authorities in their respective industries. When they endorse or engage with your brand, it enhances your credibility and builds trust among their followers. The association with a respected influencer lends credibility to your products or services, making it more likely for their audience to consider and engage with your offerings.

Finding and Partnering with LinkedIn Influencers

To effectively partner with LinkedIn influencers, follow these strategies:

Define Your Target Audience and Goals

Before identifying and approaching influencers, define your target audience and sales goals. Understand the specific demographic or industry segment you want to reach and the objectives you aim to achieve through influencer collaboration. This clarity will help you identify the most suitable influencers for your brand.

Research and Identify Relevant Influencers

Conduct thorough research to identify influencers who align with your target audience and industry. Look for influencers who create valuable content, have an engaged following, and share similar values to your brand. Consider factors such as follower size, engagement rates, and the relevance of their content to ensure an effective partnership.

Build Authentic Relationships

Approach influencers with a genuine interest in their work and a desire to collaborate. Personalize your outreach messages to demonstrate that you've done your research and understand their expertise. Engage with their content, provide meaningful comments, and share their posts to build an authentic relationship.

Co-create Valuable Content

Collaborate with influencers to co-create valuable content that resonates with their audience and promotes your brand. This could include guest blog posts, joint webinars, or featured interviews. Ensure that the content provides unique insights, adds value to the audience, and showcases your expertise.

Track and Measure Impact

Monitor the impact of your influencer collaborations using LinkedIn analytics and other tracking tools. Track metrics such as reach, engagement, website traffic, and lead generation to evaluate the success of your partnerships. This data will help you refine your influencer strategies and optimize future collaborations.

Nurturing Long-Term Relationships with Influencers

To maximize the benefits of influencer partnerships, focus on building long-term relationships. Here are some strategies for nurturing these relationships:

Provide Value to Influencers

Continuously find ways to provide value to influencers, beyond the initial collaboration. Share their content, promote their events, and provide them with exclusive access to resources or industry insights. By offering value, you strengthen your relationship and make them more likely to continue supporting your brand.

Engage and Interact

Stay engaged with influencers by regularly interacting with their content. Like, comment, and share their posts, and tag them when relevant. Engaging in meaningful conversations and providing valuable insights showcases your expertise and keeps you on their radar.

Offer Reciprocity

Consider opportunities to reciprocate the support from influencers. This could include featuring them in your content, inviting them to participate in webinars or panel discussions, or endorsing their work. By offering reciprocity, you foster a mutually beneficial relationship.

Summary

Chapter 9 of "LinkedIn Sales Mastery: Unlocking Profitable Leads and Dominating the Global Market" explores the strategies for expanding your reach with LinkedIn influencers. By partnering with influencers, you can tap into their network, gain visibility, and enhance credibility. We discussed the benefits of influencer collaborations, strategies for finding and partnering with influencers, and tips for nurturing long-term relationships. By harnessing the power of LinkedIn influencers, you can unlock profitable leads and establish dominance in the global market.

Chapter 10: Strategies for Global Expansion on LinkedIn

In this chapter, we delve into the strategies for achieving global expansion on LinkedIn and unlocking profitable leads in international markets. LinkedIn provides a powerful platform to connect with professionals worldwide and expand your reach beyond borders. To dominate the global market, it is crucial to understand the nuances of different regions, tailor your approach, and implement proven strategies for success. We will explore effective strategies and best practices for expanding your presence globally on LinkedIn.

Understanding International Markets

Before embarking on global expansion, it is essential to gain a deep understanding of the international markets you wish to target. Consider the following factors:

Cultural Differences and Localisation

Cultural differences play a significant role in shaping business practices and communication styles. Take the time to research and understand the cultural nuances of your target markets. Adapt your content and messaging to resonate with the local audience, ensuring it aligns with their preferences, values, and language.

When expanding into international markets on LinkedIn, it's crucial to recognise that cultural differences play a significant role in shaping consumer behaviour and expectations. Cultural norms, values, language, and customs vary from one country to another. To successfully penetrate new markets, businesses must understand and respect these cultural differences.

Strategies for Understanding International Markets on LinkedIn

To effectively navigate international markets on LinkedIn and maximise your global expansion efforts, consider implementing the following strategies:

1. Research and Analysis

Conduct thorough research and analysis of the target markets you plan to enter. Gain insights into the local culture, customs, language preferences, and business practices. Identify how professionals in those markets engage on LinkedIn and adapt your marketing approach accordingly.

Example:

Suppose you are a fashion brand expanding into the **Asian market**. Before launching your LinkedIn campaigns, conduct research on fashion trends, consumer preferences, and social media usage in each target country. This will help you tailor your content and messaging to resonate with the local audience, leading to higher engagement and conversion rates.

2. Localise Your Content

Localisation involves adapting your content to suit the preferences and cultural nuances of the target market. Translate your content into the local language and ensure that it is culturally relevant and resonates with the local audience. This includes using appropriate language, images, and references that align with the local culture.

Example:

Suppose you are a software company expanding into the **European market.**

Instead of using a generic marketing message, localise your LinkedIn content by translating it into the native languages of your target countries. Additionally, customise your content to reflect the unique needs and preferences of each market. This personalised approach demonstrates your commitment to understanding the local market and builds trust with your audience.

3. Engage with Local Professionals

Building relationships with local professionals is crucial for success in international markets. Engage with professionals on LinkedIn by joining industry-specific groups, participating in relevant discussions, and sharing valuable insights. This demonstrates your interest in the local market and allows you to connect with potential customers and partners.

Example:

Suppose you are a consulting firm expanding into the **Middle East market**. Engage with professionals in the region by joining LinkedIn groups focused on business and industry trends in the Middle East. Share thought-provoking articles and insights that address the specific challenges faced by businesses in the region. This positions you as an industry expert and helps establish relationships with key stakeholders.

4. Collaborate with Local Influencers

Influencer marketing can be a powerful strategy to increase your visibility and credibility in international markets. Identify influential individuals or industry experts in your target markets and collaborate with them to promote your brand and offerings. Their endorsement can significantly impact the perception of your business among the local audience.

Example:

Suppose you are a travel agency expanding into **South America**. Identify popular travel bloggers or influencers in each country and collaborate with them to showcase the unique experiences and destinations your agency offers. Their recommendations and firsthand experiences can influence the travel decisions of their followers and generate valuable leads for your business.

Market Research and Competitive Analysis

Conduct thorough market research and competitive analysis in each target region. Identify key players, market trends, and customer needs. This knowledge will help you position your offerings effectively and differentiate yourself from competitors.

Legal and Regulatory Considerations

Familiarise yourself with the legal and regulatory requirements of each target market. Ensure compliance with local laws and regulations related to data privacy, marketing, and business operations. Adhering to these requirements builds trust and credibility with your international audience. In this section, we will discuss the importance of understanding international markets' legal and regulatory considerations and provide suitable strategies and examples.

Importance of Legal and Regulatory Considerations in International Markets

Expanding your business globally on LinkedIn requires a thorough understanding of the legal and regulatory landscape in each target market. Failing to comply with local laws and regulations can result in significant setbacks and legal consequences. By proactively addressing legal and regulatory considerations, you can establish a strong foundation for success in international markets.

Strategies for Understanding International Markets' Legal and Regulatory Considerations

To navigate the legal and regulatory landscape of international markets effectively, consider implementing the following strategies:

1. Research Local Laws and Regulations

Before entering a new international market, conduct comprehensive research on the local laws and regulations that govern business operations, marketing activities, data privacy, and other relevant areas. Each country has its unique legal framework, and understanding these intricacies is crucial to ensuring compliance and building trust with potential customers.

Example:

Suppose you are a software-as-a-service (**SaaS**) provider planning to expand into the European Union (**EU**). In this case, you need to familiarize yourself with the General Data Protection Regulation (**GDPR**), which sets strict guidelines for handling and processing personal data. Ensuring your business processes and data management practices align with GDPR requirements is vital for establishing credibility and trust with EU customers.

2. Seek Legal Counsel and Expert Advice

Engage local legal counsel or consultants who specialize in international business and the target markets you wish to enter. These professionals can provide valuable insights into the legal and regulatory landscape, assist with compliance matters, and guide you through the complexities of local regulations. Their expertise can help you avoid costly mistakes and ensure that your business operates within the legal boundaries of each market.

Example:

Suppose you plan to expand into the Middle Eastern market, where cultural norms and legal systems may differ significantly from your home country. Seeking advice from local legal counsel familiar with the region's business practices and regulations can help you navigate potential challenges related to contract negotiations, intellectual property rights, or cultural sensitivities.

3. Establish Relationships with Local Partners and Networks

Building relationships with local partners, industry associations, or trade organizations can provide invaluable support in understanding the legal and regulatory considerations of a specific market. Collaborating with reputable local partners can help you gain insights, establish credibility, and navigate complex legal landscapes more effectively.

Example:

Suppose you are a fashion retailer looking to expand into the Asian market. Partnering with a local distributor who has a strong understanding of the market's legal requirements and distribution channels can help you navigate import regulations, intellectual property protection, and local customs.

Additionally, engaging with industry associations or trade organizations can provide access to resources, networking opportunities, and up-to-date information on legal and regulatory changes.

Tailoring Your LinkedIn Strategy for Global Expansion

To achieve global expansion on LinkedIn, implement the following strategies:

Multilingual Profiles and Content

Create multilingual profiles and content to cater to your international audience. Translate your profile information, posts, and articles into the local languages of your target markets. This approach demonstrates your commitment to engaging with the local community and facilitates better communication.

Localized Hashtags and Keywords

Use localized hashtags and keywords to optimize your visibility in specific regions. Research popular industry keywords and hashtags in each target market and incorporate them strategically into your content. This practice improves the discoverability of your posts among relevant audiences.

Regionalized Networking and Engagement

Build connections and engage with professionals in your target markets by actively networking with individuals and groups based in those regions. Participate in industry-specific discussions, comment on relevant posts, and share valuable insights. This approach helps you establish meaningful connections and positions you as an expert in the local industry.

Collaborate with Local Influencers

Partner with local influencers in your target markets to amplify your reach and credibility. Identify influencers who have a strong presence and following in specific regions and collaborate with them on content creation, joint webinars, or guest appearances. Their influence and local expertise will help you connect with the right audience and gain trust in the new market.

Leverage LinkedIn Advertising

Utilize LinkedIn advertising features to target specific regions and demographics. Craft targeted ad campaigns that resonate with the cultural and business preferences of your international audience. Tailor your messaging and visuals to align with the local market and drive engagement and conversions.

Tracking and Measuring Global Success

To measure the success of your global expansion efforts on LinkedIn, track and analyse key metrics:

Regional Performance Metrics

Monitor regional performance metrics, such as follower growth, engagement rates, and lead conversions, to evaluate the effectiveness of your strategies in each target market. Identify regions that are performing well and areas where you may need to adjust your approach.

Language-specific Engagement

Analyse engagement levels and interactions across different languages to understand which languages are resonating most with your international audience. Use this insight to optimize your multilingual content strategy and focus on languages that drive the highest engagement. This section focuses on the importance of language-specific engagement and provides strategies for effectively reaching and connecting with diverse audiences across different countries and cultures.

Strategies for Language-specific Engagement - Understanding International Markets

To successfully engage with international markets on LinkedIn, consider implementing the following strategies:

1. Localize Your Content

Localization is the process of adapting your content to suit the language, cultural nuances, and preferences of your target audience in different regions. Translate your LinkedIn profile, posts, and articles into the languages spoken in your target markets. Ensure that the translated content is not only accurate but also culturally appropriate and resonates with the local audience.

Example:

Suppose you are a fashion retailer expanding your presence into the Spanish market. Localize your LinkedIn content by translating your product descriptions, promotional posts, and customer testimonials into Spanish. This approach enables you to connect with Spanish-speaking audiences on a deeper level and positions your brand as one that understands their preferences and needs.

2. Research Cultural Differences

Different cultures have unique communication styles, etiquette, and business practices. Before engaging with international markets, invest time in researching and understanding the cultural differences of your target regions. This knowledge will help you tailor your messaging and approach to be culturally sensitive and appropriate.

Example:

When expanding into the **Japanese market**, it is important to be aware of their business customs. In Japan, relationships are built on trust and respect, and direct selling approaches may not be well-received. Take the time to understand the Japanese business culture, adapt your communication style accordingly, and focus on building relationships before promoting your products or services.

3. Collaborate with Local Influencers

Engaging with local influencers can significantly boost your reach and credibility in international markets. Identify influential individuals or thought leaders in your target regions who align with your brand values and have a substantial following. Collaborate with them to promote your content or endorse your products/services to their audience. This can help you gain trust and credibility among the local community.

Example:
Suppose you are a technology company entering the Indian market. Collaborate with well-known technology influencers in India to endorse your products or share your content with their followers. Their endorsement can significantly increase your visibility and attract a relevant audience who values their opinions.

4. Leverage LinkedIn's Language Targeting

LinkedIn provides language targeting options for ads, allowing you to reach users who have specified their preferred language on their profiles. Utilize this feature to tailor your ad campaigns specifically to users who understand a particular language.

Example:

Suppose you are a language learning platform targeting **Spanish-speaking** professionals. Set your language targeting to Spanish so that your ads are shown to users who have indicated Spanish as their preferred language on their LinkedIn profiles. This ensures that your ads are reaching the right audience and increases the likelihood of engagement.

By implementing these strategies for language-specific engagement and understanding international markets, you can effectively expand your reach and establish meaningful connections with diverse audiences around the globe on LinkedIn. Remember to adapt your approach to the cultural preferences and communication styles of each target market to maximize your success.

Conversion Rates and Revenue Generation

Track conversion rates and revenue generated from your global LinkedIn efforts. Assess the return on investment (ROI) for each target market and identify areas for improvement. This data will help you allocate resources effectively and refine your strategies.

Summary

Chapter 10 of "LinkedIn Sales Mastery: Unlocking Profitable Leads and Dominating the Global Market" provides strategies for global expansion on LinkedIn. Understanding international markets, tailoring your LinkedIn strategy, and tracking key metrics are crucial steps in unlocking profitable leads and dominating the global market. By implementing these proven strategies, you can successfully expand your presence across borders and establish a strong foothold in international markets.

Chapter 11: Advanced Networking Techniques for LinkedIn Success

In this chapter, we explore advanced networking techniques that can take your LinkedIn success to new heights. Networking is a crucial aspect of building relationships, expanding your professional circle, and unlocking profitable leads on LinkedIn. By implementing proven strategies and leveraging advanced techniques, you can maximise the potential of your network and establish yourself as a trusted authority in your industry. We will delve into the intricacies of advanced networking and provide practical tips for LinkedIn success.

Building Meaningful Connections

Creating meaningful connections is the foundation of successful networking on LinkedIn. Here are some strategies to build authentic relationships:

Personalised Connection Requests

When sending connection requests, take the time to personalise your message. Mention why you want to connect and highlight any common interests or shared connections. This personalised approach demonstrates your genuine interest and increases the likelihood of a positive response.

Engaging with Content

Engage with the content shared by your connections and industry influencers. Like, comment, and share their posts to showcase your active involvement and contribute valuable insights to the conversation. Engaging with content fosters meaningful connections and establishes you as a thought leader.

Participating in LinkedIn Groups

Join relevant LinkedIn groups and actively participate in discussions. Share your expertise, answer questions, and provide valuable insights to position yourself as a valuable member of the community. Engaging in group activities opens doors to new connections and opportunities. In this section, we will discuss effective strategies for participating in LinkedIn Groups and provide relevant examples.

Strategies for Participating in LinkedIn Groups

To make the most of your participation in LinkedIn Groups and unlock networking opportunities, consider implementing the following strategies:

1. Identify and Join Relevant Groups

Start by identifying LinkedIn Groups that align with your professional interests, industry, or target audience. Look for groups where your target prospects, industry thought leaders or potential collaborators are active. Joining these groups allows you to connect with like-minded professionals and engage in conversations that are relevant to your niche.

Example:

Suppose you are a marketing consultant specializing in the hospitality industry. Look for LinkedIn Groups dedicated to hospitality professionals, hotel management, or travel industry marketing. By joining these groups, you can engage with professionals in the industry, share your expertise, and build relationships with potential clients or referral partners.

2. Be Active and Engage in Discussions

Actively participate in group discussions by sharing valuable insights, asking thought-provoking questions, and contributing to conversations. This helps establish your expertise and credibility within the group. Be responsive to other members' comments and questions, and provide helpful and informative responses.

Example:

Suppose you are a social media strategist participating in a LinkedIn Group for digital marketers. Engage in discussions by sharing tips on leveraging social media platforms, discussing the latest industry trends, and providing insights on effective campaign strategies. By consistently contributing valuable content, you position yourself as a go-to resource in your area of expertise and attract the attention of potential clients or collaborators.

3. Provide Value through Content Sharing

LinkedIn Groups offer an excellent opportunity to share relevant content and resources with group members. Share articles, blog posts, infographics, or industry reports that provide valuable insights and solutions to common challenges. By sharing valuable content, you position yourself as a knowledgeable professional and gain visibility within the group.

Example:

Suppose you are a cybersecurity expert participating in a LinkedIn Group for IT professionals. Share informative articles on emerging cybersecurity threats, tips for securing sensitive data, or case studies highlighting successful cybersecurity implementations. By sharing valuable content, you establish yourself as a trusted authority in the field, and group members are more likely to reach out to you for further discussions or potential business collaborations.

4. Network and Connect with Group Members

One of the primary goals of participating in LinkedIn Groups is to expand your network. Take the opportunity to connect with group members who align with your professional goals or are potential clients, partners, or industry influencers. Send personalized connection requests highlighting common interests or the value you can bring to their network.

Example:

Suppose you are a freelance graphic designer participating in a LinkedIn Group for creative professionals. Identify individuals who may require your design services or who are influential in the industry. Send them a personalized connection request mentioning your appreciation for their work and your interest in connecting to explore potential collaborations. This personalized approach increases the likelihood of building meaningful connections.

5. Be Respectful and Professional

When participating in LinkedIn Groups, maintain a professional and respectful tone in your interactions. Avoid engaging in heated debates or posting controversial content that may negatively impact your professional reputation. Aim to add value to discussions, offer constructive feedback, and be supportive of fellow group members.

Example:

Suppose you are a marketing consultant participating in a LinkedIn Group discussing branding strategies. If you come across a post where someone is seeking feedback on their logo design, provide constructive criticism and suggestions for improvement rather than resorting to negative comments. By demonstrating your professionalism and respectful attitude, you enhance your credibility and build positive relationships within the group. Remember, the key to success in participating in LinkedIn Groups is to actively engage, provide value, and build authentic relationships with other professionals. By following these strategies, you can leverage the power of LinkedIn Groups to expand your network, establish your expertise, and uncover new business opportunities.

Leveraging Advanced Search and Filters

LinkedIn's advanced search and filtering capabilities can significantly enhance your networking efforts. Here's how to leverage them effectively:

Advanced Search Queries

Utilise advanced search queries to narrow down your search for specific professionals, companies, or industries. Customise your search parameters based on criteria such as location, job title, industry, and company size. This targeted approach helps you find relevant connections with precision. In this section, we will discuss strategies for using advanced search queries on LinkedIn and provide relevant examples.

Strategies for Using Advanced Search Queries

To maximize your networking success on LinkedIn, consider implementing the following strategies for using advanced search queries:

1. Specify Keywords and Phrases

When conducting an advanced search on LinkedIn, be specific with the keywords and phrases you use. Instead of using generic terms, focus on industry-specific keywords, job titles, skills, or other relevant criteria that align with your networking goals.

Example:

Suppose you are a marketing consultant specializing in social media. Instead of searching for "**marketing**" or "**social media,**" use more specific terms like "**social media strategy,**" "**content marketing,**" or "**social media manager.**" These targeted keywords will help you find professionals who are specifically interested in or working in those areas, increasing the relevance of your networking efforts.

2. Utilize Boolean Operators

LinkedIn's advanced search allows you to use Boolean operators to refine your search queries. These operators include AND, OR, and NOT, and they can be used to combine or exclude specific terms from your search.

- **AND**: Use the AND operator to find profiles that include multiple terms.

For example, "**social media AND marketing**" will yield results that include both terms.

- **OR**: Use the OR operator to broaden your search by including profiles that contain either of the specified terms. For example, "**social media OR digital marketing**" will provide results for profiles with either term.
- **NOT**: Use the NOT operator to exclude specific terms from your search results. For example, "**social media NOT manager**" will exclude profiles with the term "**manager.**"

By using Boolean operators, you can refine your search queries and find professionals who match your specific criteria more accurately.

3. Refine Filters and Parameters

LinkedIn's advanced search also allows you to refine your search results further by applying various filters and parameters. These include location, industry, company size, seniority level, and more. Refining your search with these filters helps you target professionals who are most relevant to your networking goals.

Example:

Suppose you are looking to connect with marketing professionals in the healthcare industry. You can use LinkedIn's advanced search to filter the results based on the industry **"Healthcare"** and job titles like **"Marketing Manager"** or **"Marketing Director."** This allows you to narrow down your search and focus on professionals in the specific industry and roles you are interested in.

Saved Searches and Alerts

Save your frequently used search queries and set up alerts to stay updated on new results. LinkedIn will notify you when new profiles match your search criteria, allowing you to proactively reach out to potential connections. Saved searches and alerts streamline your networking process and save time.

Filters and Recommendations

Use filters and recommendations to discover new connections. LinkedIn suggests relevant professionals based on your existing network and search history. Explore these recommendations and apply filters to refine your search and uncover hidden networking opportunities.

Networking Etiquette and Relationship Building

Networking etiquette and relationship building are crucial for long-term success on LinkedIn. Follow these best practices:

Personalised Messages and Follow-ups

When reaching out to new connections or following up with existing ones, send personalised messages. Reference previous conversations or interactions to demonstrate your attentiveness and interest. Personalised messages show that you value the relationship and enhance the likelihood of continued engagement.

Offering Value and Support

Actively look for ways to offer value and support to your connections. Share relevant industry insights, provide introductions to valuable contacts, or endorse their skills and expertise. By being helpful and supportive, you strengthen your relationships and foster a reciprocal network.

Maintaining Consistent Engagement

Consistency is key to successful networking. Regularly engage with your connections by liking, commenting, and sharing their content. Send periodic messages to check in, congratulate them on achievements, or share relevant resources. Consistent engagement keeps your connections active and strengthens the bond.

Leveraging LinkedIn Events and Webinars

LinkedIn Events and Webinars offer powerful networking opportunities. Here's how to make the most of them:

Hosting Your Own Events

Host virtual events or webinars on LinkedIn to showcase your expertise and attract industry professionals. Deliver valuable content, invite influential speakers, and actively engage with participants. Hosting events establishes you as a thought leader and creates networking opportunities with attendees.

Participating in Industry Events

Attend and actively participate in industry events and webinars organised by others. Network with participants, ask insightful questions and share your expertise. Active participation positions you as an engaged industry professional and opens doors for collaboration and new connections.

Summary

Chapter 11 of "LinkedIn Sales Mastery: Unlocking Profitable Leads and Dominating the Global Market" explores advanced networking techniques for LinkedIn success. By building meaningful connections, leveraging advanced search and filters, practising networking etiquette, and leveraging LinkedIn Events and Webinars, you can elevate your networking efforts and unlock new opportunities. Implement these proven strategies to expand your network, establish valuable relationships, and dominate the global market on LinkedIn.

Chapter 12: LinkedIn as a Sales Funnel: From Lead to Conversion

In this final chapter of "LinkedIn Sales Mastery: Unlocking Profitable Leads and Dominating the Global Market," we delve into the powerful role LinkedIn plays as a sales funnel, guiding leads through the conversion process. LinkedIn provides a unique opportunity to engage with potential customers, build relationships, and ultimately drive conversions. By implementing proven strategies and leveraging the platform's features, you can optimise your sales funnel and achieve greater success on LinkedIn. Let's explore the techniques that will help you convert leads into loyal customers.

Optimising Your LinkedIn Profile for Conversion

Your LinkedIn profile is your virtual storefront, and it plays a crucial role in capturing and converting leads. Here are some strategies to optimise it for maximum impact:

1. Clear and Compelling Headline

Craft a clear and compelling headline that immediately communicates your value proposition. Use keywords and phrases that resonate with your target audience and highlight the benefits they can expect from working with you. A strong headline captures attention and entices potential customers to explore further.

2. Engaging Summary

Write an engaging summary that showcases your expertise, experience, and unique selling points. Use storytelling techniques to captivate readers and demonstrate how you can address their pain points and provide solutions. Show your personality and let your passion shine through to create a memorable impression.

3. Showcase Relevant Experience and Achievements

Highlight your relevant experience, accomplishments, and certifications. This builds credibility and establishes trust with potential customers. Use concise and compelling language to demonstrate your expertise and track record of success. Include specific examples and metrics whenever possible to quantify your achievements.

Engaging with Leads

To move leads through the sales funnel, it's important to engage with them effectively. Here's how to do it:

1. Personalised Messaging

When reaching out to leads, avoid generic messages and opt for personalised ones instead. Reference specific details from their profile or previous interactions to show genuine interest. Tailor your message to their needs and demonstrate how your product or service can solve their pain points. Personalisation creates a connection and increases the chances of a positive response.

2. Timely Follow-ups

Follow up promptly and consistently with your leads. Don't let potential opportunities slip away due to delays. Set reminders and establish a system to ensure timely follow-ups. Be persistent without being pushy, and always provide value in your communications.

3. Building Relationships

LinkedIn is not just a platform for sales pitches; it's a place to build relationships. Engage with your leads by liking, commenting, and sharing their content. Offer helpful insights and advice, and demonstrate your expertise by providing value. Building authentic relationships establishes trust and lays the foundation for long-term customer loyalty.

Leveraging LinkedIn Features for Conversion

LinkedIn offers a range of features that can enhance your conversion efforts. Here are some key features to leverage:

1. Showcase Pages

Create Showcase Pages to highlight specific products, services, or business segments. These dedicated pages allow you to tailor your messaging and engage with leads who have specific interests or needs. Showcase Pages provide a focused platform for targeted conversion. In this section, we will discuss strategies for leveraging Showcase Pages to drive conversions and provide relevant examples.

Strategies for Leveraging Showcase Pages for Conversion

To maximize the effectiveness of Showcase Pages and convert leads into customers, consider implementing the following strategies:

1. Highlight Specific Offerings

Showcase Pages allow you to create dedicated pages for specific products or services. Use this opportunity to highlight the unique features, benefits, and value propositions of each offering. By providing detailed information and compelling content about your products or services, you can capture the interest of your target audience and drive them towards conversion.

Example:

Suppose you run a digital marketing agency offering various services such as search engine optimization (SEO), social media marketing, and content creation. Create separate Showcase Pages for each service and focus on showcasing the specific benefits and success stories related to that particular service. This targeted approach enables you to engage with leads who are specifically interested in a particular service and increase the likelihood of conversion.

2. Engage with Relevant Content

Engaging content plays a crucial role in driving conversions. Share valuable and relevant content on your Showcase

Pages to educate, inform, and inspire your target audience. This content can include blog posts, case studies, videos, infographics, and industry insights. By consistently providing high-quality content, you establish your authority in the field and build trust with your audience, increasing the likelihood of conversion.

Example:

Continuing with the digital marketing agency example, you can share blog posts on your Showcase Pages that offer tips and best practices for improving SEO, increasing social media engagement, or creating compelling content. This content demonstrates your expertise and provides value to your audience, positioning your agency as a trusted resource and increasing the chances of converting leads into customers.

3. Utilize Call-to-Action Buttons

LinkedIn Showcase Pages offer call-to-action (CTA) buttons that can be customized to align with your conversion goals. Take advantage of these CTAs by directing your audience to take specific actions that lead to conversion. Whether it's signing up for a free trial, requesting a consultation, or making a purchase, the CTA buttons provide a clear and direct path for your audience to take the desired action.

Example:

If you run an e-commerce store, you can use the CTA button on your Showcase Page to direct visitors to your product page or encourage them to make a purchase with a limited-time discount code. This streamlined approach removes friction and guides your audience towards conversion.

4. Monitor Analytics and Refine Strategies

LinkedIn provides analytics for Showcase Pages, allowing you to track the performance of your content and campaigns. Monitor key metrics such as engagement, click-through rates, and conversion rates to evaluate the effectiveness of your strategies. Use these insights to refine your content, CTAs, and overall approach to continually optimize your Showcase Pages for better conversion rates.

Example:

Suppose you notice that a specific type of content, such as video tutorials or customer testimonials, generates higher engagement and conversion rates on your Showcase Page. Based on this insight, you can create more of such content or adjust your content strategy to focus on what resonates best with your audience, increasing the chances of converting leads into customers.

In conclusion, Showcase Pages offer an excellent opportunity to leverage LinkedIn's features for conversion. By highlighting specific offerings, providing engaging content, utilizing call-to-action buttons, and monitoring analytics, you can optimize your Showcase Pages to drive conversions and achieve long-term success.

2. LinkedIn InMail

LinkedIn InMail allows you to send direct messages to potential leads who are not in your network. Craft compelling and personalised messages to grab their attention and drive them towards conversion. Use InMail strategically to nurture leads and guide them through the sales funnel. In this section, we will discuss strategies for leveraging LinkedIn InMail and maximizing conversions, accompanied by relevant examples.

Strategies for Leveraging LinkedIn InMail for Conversion

To make the most of LinkedIn InMail and enhance your conversion rates, consider implementing the following strategies:

A. Personalization is Key

When reaching out to prospects via LinkedIn InMail, personalization plays a crucial role in capturing their attention and fostering engagement. Craft tailored messages that address the specific needs, challenges, or goals of each prospect. Reference their professional background, recent activities, or mutual connections to establish a connection and demonstrate that you have taken the time to research and understand their situation.

Example:

Suppose you are a digital marketing agency reaching out to potential clients in the healthcare industry. In your InMail, you can mention a recent industry conference they attended or a blog post they published related to healthcare marketing. By showing that you have a genuine interest in their work and an understanding of their industry, you increase the likelihood of receiving a positive response and moving towards conversion.

B. Focus on Value Proposition

In your LinkedIn InMail messages, clearly communicate the unique value proposition of your product or service. Highlight the specific benefits and outcomes that prospects can expect by engaging with your offering. This helps to differentiate your solution from competitors and gives prospects a compelling reason to consider your proposal.

Example:

Suppose you are a software company offering a project management tool. In your InMail, you can emphasize how your tool streamlines project workflows, increases team collaboration and improves overall productivity. By showcasing the tangible benefits and addressing pain points commonly experienced in project management, you position your solution as a valuable resource and increase the likelihood of conversion.

C. Call-to-Action (CTA)

Include a clear and concise call-to-action in your LinkedIn InMail messages to prompt prospects to take the desired next step. Whether it's scheduling a call, requesting a demo, or visiting a specific landing page, provide a direct pathway for prospects to engage further with your offering. A well-crafted CTA encourages prospects to take action and facilitates the conversion process.

Example:

In your InMail, you can conclude with a CTA such as, **"I would love to discuss how our solution can help you achieve [specific goal]. Let's**

schedule a brief call at your convenience. Are you available next week?" By providing a specific action to take and expressing your availability, you make it easier for prospects to respond and move closer to conversion.

D. Follow-up and Relationship Building

LinkedIn InMail provides an opportunity to initiate conversations and begin building relationships with prospects. However, the conversion process often requires multiple touchpoints. Follow up with prospects who have shown interest or engaged with your initial message. Continue the conversation by sharing relevant content, offering further insights, or addressing any questions or concerns they may have. Building a relationship over time increases trust and the likelihood of conversion.

Example:

Suppose you have sent an InMail introducing your consulting services to a prospect. If they respond positively or show interest, you can follow up with additional information, such as a case study showcasing how you have helped similar clients achieve their goals. This reinforces your expertise and demonstrates the value you can provide, nurturing the relationship and moving towards conversion.

3. LinkedIn Ads

LinkedIn Ads offer powerful targeting options to reach your ideal audience. Create compelling ad campaigns that resonate with your target market and lead them towards conversion. Experiment with different ad formats and messaging to find what works best for your specific goals. In this section, we will discuss strategies for leveraging LinkedIn ads to optimize your sales funnel and provide relevant examples.

Strategies for LinkedIn Ads

To make the most of your LinkedIn ads and maximize lead conversion, consider implementing the following strategies:

1. Define Your Advertising Goals

Before launching your LinkedIn ad campaign, it's essential to define your advertising goals. What do you want to achieve with your ads? Are you looking to generate leads, increase website traffic, promote a specific product or service, or raise brand awareness? By clearly defining your goals, you can align your ad campaign with your desired outcomes and measure its effectiveness.

Example:

Suppose you are a B2B marketing agency aiming to generate leads for your content marketing services. Your advertising goal could be to drive qualified leads to a landing page where prospects can sign up for a free consultation. By defining this goal, you can structure your ads and landing page to encourage lead generation.

2. Tailor Your Ad Content to Your Target Audience

To effectively engage your target audience, it's crucial to tailor your ad content to their needs and preferences. Craft compelling ad copy and design eye-catching visuals that resonate with your audience. Highlight the unique value proposition of your product or service and explain how it can address their pain points or fulfil their desires. Personalisation and relevance are key to capturing your audience's attention and encouraging them to take action.

Example:

Suppose you are a SaaS company offering project management software to small businesses. In your LinkedIn ad, you can emphasise how your software simplifies project collaboration, streamlines workflows, and improves team productivity. Targeting small business owners or project managers, you can highlight the specific challenges they face and position your software as the solution to their problems.

3. Segment and Test Your Ads

Segmenting your target audience and testing different ad variations are crucial steps in optimizing your LinkedIn ad campaign. Divide your audience into segments based on demographics, job titles, industries, or other relevant criteria. Then, create multiple ad variations for each segment and test their performance. This allows you to identify which ads resonate best with each segment and refine your campaign accordingly.

Example:

Suppose you are a marketing automation platform targeting both small businesses and enterprise-level companies. In your ad campaign, you can create different ad sets for each segment and test variations in ad copy, visuals, or calls to action. By monitoring the performance of each ad set, you can gather insights on what resonates best with each audience segment and adjust your campaign to improve conversions.

4. Track and Analyse Campaign Performance

Tracking and analysing the performance of your LinkedIn ad campaign is essential for optimizing your sales funnel. Use LinkedIn's ad analytics tools to monitor key metrics such as impressions, clicks, conversions, and cost per conversion. Identify the ads and audience segments that are driving the most significant results and allocate your budget accordingly. Continuously analyse the data and make data-driven adjustments to improve the effectiveness of your campaign.

Example:

Suppose you are running a LinkedIn ad campaign to promote a new e-commerce platform. By tracking the performance metrics, you discover that ad set A targeting retail businesses generates a higher click-through rate and conversion rate compared to ad set B targeting service-based businesses. With this information, you can allocate more budget to ad set A and refine your targeting strategies to capture more qualified leads.

By implementing these strategies, you can effectively leverage LinkedIn ads as part of your sales funnel, moving leads through the conversion process and ultimately achieving sales success. Remember to regularly evaluate and refine your ad campaign based on the data and insights gathered, ensuring that you are continuously improving your results.

Monitoring and Optimising Your Sales Funnel

To ensure continuous improvement, it's essential to monitor and optimise your sales funnel. Here's how to do it effectively:

1. Tracking Key Metrics

Identify key metrics to track and measure the performance of your sales funnel. These may include conversion rates, click-through rates, engagement levels, and lead quality. Regularly analyse the data and make data-driven decisions to improve your conversion rates.

2. A/B Testing

Conduct A/B testing to refine your messaging, visuals, and calls to action. Test different variations of your landing pages, ads, and email campaigns to identify the most effective elements. Make incremental improvements based on the results to continually optimise your conversion process.

3. Customer Feedback and Surveys

Seek feedback from your customers to understand their experience throughout the sales funnel. Use surveys or direct conversations to gather insights into their pain points, preferences, and areas for improvement. Incorporate their feedback to enhance the overall customer journey and increase conversions.

Summary

Chapter 12 of "LinkedIn Sales Mastery: Unlocking Profitable Leads and Dominating the Global Market" explores the power of LinkedIn as a sales funnel, guiding leads from initial contact to conversion. By optimising your LinkedIn profile, engaging with leads effectively, leveraging LinkedIn features, and monitoring and optimising your sales funnel, you can drive conversions and achieve greater success on LinkedIn. Implement these proven strategies to maximise your lead-to-conversion process and dominate the global market on LinkedIn.

FAQs

Q1: What is the importance of LinkedIn in the sales process? LinkedIn plays a crucial role in the sales process as it provides a platform for professionals to connect, build relationships, and generate leads. With its vast network of professionals, LinkedIn offers unparalleled opportunities for targeting and engaging with potential customers.

Q2: How can I optimize my LinkedIn profile to attract leads? To optimize your LinkedIn profile, ensure that it is complete, professional, and showcases your expertise. Use a compelling headline, include relevant keywords, and highlight your achievements and experience. Additionally, add a captivating profile picture and engage with industry-specific content to build credibility.

Q3: How can I effectively search for prospects on LinkedIn? Utilize LinkedIn's advanced search filters to target prospects based on specific criteria such as job title, industry, location, and company size. Refine your searches to find the most relevant leads and leverage LinkedIn Sales Navigator for even more advanced search capabilities.

Q4: What are some effective strategies for engaging with potential customers on LinkedIn? Engage with potential customers by sharing valuable content, participating in relevant industry groups, and commenting on posts. Personalize your interactions and demonstrate a genuine interest in their needs. Building relationships through meaningful engagement is key to converting leads into customers.

Q5: How can I leverage LinkedIn groups for networking and lead generation? Join relevant LinkedIn groups in your industry or target market and actively participate by sharing valuable insights, answering questions, and networking with group members. By establishing yourself as a knowledgeable resource, you can generate leads and expand your network.

Q6: What are the benefits of using LinkedIn Sales Navigator? LinkedIn Sales Navigator provides advanced search features, lead recommendations, and insights to help you find and connect with your ideal prospects. It allows you to track and engage with leads more effectively, enhancing your overall sales strategy.

Q7: How can I create compelling content on LinkedIn to attract leads? Create content that addresses the pain points and challenges of your target audience. Offer valuable insights, share success stories, and provide actionable tips. Use a mix of formats such as articles, videos, and infographics to engage your audience.

Q8: Is it beneficial to invest in LinkedIn advertising for lead generation? LinkedIn advertising can be highly effective for lead generation, especially when targeting specific industries or job roles. Sponsored content, sponsored InMail, and text ads are some of the advertising options that can help you reach a wider audience and generate quality leads.

Q9: How can I measure the success of my LinkedIn sales efforts? Track key metrics such as profile views, connection requests, engagement on posts, and conversions. LinkedIn provides analytics tools to help you monitor and evaluate the effectiveness of your sales activities.

Q10: What are some effective ways to nurture relationships with LinkedIn connections? Stay connected with your LinkedIn connections by engaging with their content, sending personalized messages, and offering support or assistance when relevant. Building meaningful relationships fosters trust and increases the likelihood of converting connections into customers.

Q11: How can LinkedIn analytics help in refining my sales strategy? LinkedIn analytics provide insights into the performance of your content, audience demographics, and engagement metrics. By analyzing this data, you can identify trends, refine your messaging, and make data-driven decisions to optimize your sales strategy.

Q12: How can I leverage LinkedIn endorsements and recommendations to enhance credibility? Encourage your connections to endorse your skills and write recommendations for your profile. These endorsements and recommendations serve as social proof, enhancing your credibility and building trust with potential customers.

Q13: How can I use LinkedIn to expand my reach globally? Join international groups, connect with professionals from different countries, and share content that is relevant to a global audience. Engaging with a diverse range of professionals can help you expand your network and tap into international business opportunities.

Q14: How can I leverage LinkedIn Pulse for content distribution?

Publish articles on LinkedIn Pulse to reach a wider audience and establish yourself as a thought leader in your industry. Promote your articles on other social media platforms and engage with readers to spark conversations and generate leads.

Q15: Can LinkedIn help me find referral partners or collaborators?

LinkedIn is an excellent platform for finding referral partners or collaborators. Search for professionals in complementary industries or those who target the same audience. Engage with them, build relationships, and explore partnership opportunities.

Q16: How can I effectively use LinkedIn messaging for lead nurturing? Personalize your LinkedIn messages based on the recipient's profile and needs. Avoid generic messages and focus on building a rapport. Share valuable content, offer assistance, and schedule calls or meetings to nurture leads through the messaging feature.

Q17: What are some best practices for connecting with potential customers on LinkedIn? When connecting with potential customers, always personalize your invitation message, explain why you'd like to connect and highlight the value you can provide. Avoid sending generic connection requests as they are less likely to be accepted.

Q18: How can I leverage LinkedIn Showcase Pages for targeted marketing? LinkedIn Showcase Pages allow you to create dedicated pages for specific products, services, or business segments. Use them to tailor your messaging and content for different target audiences, providing more focused and targeted marketing.

Q19: How can I leverage LinkedIn events for lead generation? Create and promote LinkedIn events to attract potential customers. Share valuable event information, engage with attendees, and use the event as an opportunity to generate leads and establish connections with interested prospects.

Q20: How can I effectively use LinkedIn recommendations in my sales process? Request recommendations from satisfied customers or clients on LinkedIn to showcase social proof. Display these recommendations on your profile to enhance your credibility and influence potential customers' buying decisions.

Q21: What are some effective ways to build authority and thought leadership on LinkedIn? Publish valuable content, engage in industry discussions, participate in LinkedIn groups, and share insights from your expertise. Consistency and providing valuable insights will help establish you as a trusted authority in your field.

Q22: How can I leverage LinkedIn Sales Navigator to track and manage leads effectively? Use LinkedIn Sales

Navigator to track leads, receive alerts when they engage with your content, and access valuable insights about their activity. Utilize features like Lead Lists and CRM integrations to efficiently manage your leads.

Q23: How can I effectively use LinkedIn videos for lead generation? Create engaging and informative videos that address your target audience's pain points or provide valuable insights. Share these videos on LinkedIn, optimize them with relevant keywords, and encourage engagement and sharing to generate leads.

Q24: Can LinkedIn be used for B2C sales or is it primarily for B2B? While LinkedIn is primarily known for B2B networking and sales, it can also be utilized for B2C sales. Depending on your target audience and industry, you can still connect with potential customers, share relevant content, and generate leads.

Q25: How can I leverage LinkedIn's "People Also Viewed" feature for lead generation? Explore the "People Also Viewed" section on the profiles of your target audience or connections. This feature can help you discover potential leads who share similar profiles or interests with your existing connections.

Q26: How can I use LinkedIn groups to establish myself as an industry expert? Participate actively in LinkedIn groups by sharing valuable insights, answering questions, and providing helpful resources. Consistently contribute to group discussions and showcase your expertise to establish yourself as an industry expert.

Q27: How can I generate leads through LinkedIn content advertising? LinkedIn content advertising allows you to promote your valuable content to a targeted audience. By offering valuable resources, such as e-books, webinars, or whitepapers, you can attract leads and collect their contact information for further follow-up.

Q28: How can I track the ROI of my LinkedIn advertising campaigns? LinkedIn provides robust analytics and reporting tools to track the performance of your advertising campaigns. Monitor metrics such as impressions, clicks, conversions, and cost per lead to measure the ROI of your LinkedIn advertising efforts.

Q29: How can I leverage LinkedIn's "Who's Viewed Your Profile" feature for lead generation? Review the profiles of professionals who have viewed your profile and identify potential leads. Reach out to them with personalized messages, highlighting your shared interests or potential opportunities for collaboration.

Q30: How can I use LinkedIn to enhance my personal brand as a sales professional? Consistently share valuable content, engage with industry thought leaders, and participate in relevant conversations. Build a strong professional network and showcase your expertise to enhance your personal brand as a sales professional on LinkedIn.

www.ingramcontent.com/pod-product-compliance
Lightning Source LLC
Chambersburg PA
CBHW060410220526
45465CB00008B/2827